California Real Estate
Exam Cram Workbook

Fourth Edition

ALLIED
REAL ESTATE SCHOOLS
A Division of Allied Business Schools

This publication is designed to provide accurate and current information regarding the subject matter covered. The principles and conclusions presented are subject to local, state, and federal laws and regulations, court cases, and revisions of same. If legal advice or other expert assistance is required, the reader is urged to consult a competent professional in the field.

Real Estate Publisher
Leigh Conway

Academic Information Analyst
Laura King

Writers
Ben Hernandez, Technical Writer
Sue Carlson, Technical Writer

Production Designer
Susan Mackessy Richmond

Published by
Allied Real Estate Schools
22952 Alcalde Drive
Laguna Hills, California 92653

Printed in the United States of America

ISBN: 978-1-942219-02-6

Table of Contents

ABOUT THE INSTRUCTORS

Thomas L. Jensen

Tom Jensen brings a rich background in real estate to the creation and production of this material. He is a licensed real estate broker in Texas and specializes in residential brokerage, commercial brokerage and leasing, as well as business brokerage. In 2003, Mr. Jensen established SunWest REALTORS, providing real estate services in north Texas and the Metroplex. Mr. Jensen has written and taught several real estate courses. His classroom and field experience contributed to the practical information in this workbook and DVD.

Mr. Jensen has a Bachelor's Degree in Applied Arts and Sciences from the University of North Texas. He has a Certified Real Estate Instructor (CREI) designation from the Texas Real Estate Teacher's Association. In addition, he is approved by the Texas Real Estate Commission to teach Continuing Education (CE) and Sales Agent Apprentice Education (SAE).

Sherry Price

Sherry Price is a licensed real estate broker in California and has over twenty-five years in the real estate profession include eight years of specialization in investment properties and residential sales. She has used her extensive knowledge to teach real estate classes, write several California real estate licensing textbooks, and write test questions for state licensing examinations in Nevada, Wisconsin, Minnesota, Maryland, and Iowa.

Ms. Price has a Bachelor of Science degree in Education from Long Beach State College and a California Community College Lifetime Instructor Credential.

ACKNOWLEDGEMENTS

Allied Business Schools, Inc. thanks the following people who were involved in the technical production of the California Real Estate Exam Cram DVD:

Karen Achenbach, Mary Achenbach, Jeff Samuelson, Steve Miles, John Hoffhines, Stephen Myers, Cindy Parisotto, Rick Santizo, Sang Lee, Tim Maloney, Ralph Smith, Andrew Gauvreau, Miriam Cutler, Jimmy Hammer, Steve Karman, Bruce Kasson, Peter Angeles, Marilyn Taylor, Laura King, Marley Powell; **Different By Design** – Matt Radecki, Greg Lanesey; **Alpha Dogs, Inc.** – Paul De Cham, Terry Curren, Sean Williams; and **New Constellation Technologies**.

How to Use This Workbook

Allied's California Real Estate Exam Cram Workbook/DVD tutorial is structured into two parts—the National Portion and the California Portion. The National Portion covers general real estate principles and practices, essentials of finance, real property appraisal, and real estate math. The California Portion covers California real property and licensing laws and practices specific to California.

Studied together, they will help you pass your California state licensing exam.

This workbook is designed for you to use while you are watching the Exam Cram tutorial. Follow along in your workbook as the instructor takes you through each topic. Feel free to take notes in your workbook; ample space is provided.

For your convenience, the multiple-choice questions at the end of each section are followed by an answer key.

Tips to Pass Your Real Estate License Exam

Watch Out for the Little Words

First, carefully read the words in each question and look for words like "not" and "except." These words change the whole meaning of the question. The word "except" is easy to miss, because it is usually the last word of the question. If you miss the word "except", it is impossible to answer the question correctly.

Sometimes, in the state real estate license exam, words like "not" and "except" are CAPITALIZED or in **bold print** or <u>underlined</u> in the question. This helps you to see the words, and makes it harder to misread the question.

Also, pay attention to words like "least", "most", "only", "always", and "never." These words all qualify the question, so be sure to look for these words in the question.

Read All of the Answer Choices

Next, be sure to read the answer choices carefully.

> For example, you are very confident that you have memorized the fact that there are 43,560 square feet in an acre, and the question in front of you asks, "Which of the following parcels of land equals an acre?" You think you know this one for sure, so when you see "Choice A – Parcel depth is 247.5 feet and parcel width is 176 feet", you select it. You select it because the result is 43,560 square feet.

> Unfortunately, you have just answered the question wrong . . . and that was one you absolutely should have gotten right!

> Why is the answer choice wrong? In this case, "Choices B and C" used different examples, but had the same result of 43,560 square feet. Be careful to look at all the possible answer choices that are given, before making your final selection. Sometimes the answer choice may be "Choice D – All of the Above."

So, let's get ready! Get your workbook in front of you, get something to write with, get comfortable, and you'll soon be ready to pass this test!

Exam Cram Workbook - Part 1: National Portion

Chapter 1
Property, Estates, & Ownership

BUNDLE OF RIGHTS

Property rights are known as the bundle of rights. The **bundle of rights** consists of all legal rights that are attached to the ownership of real property. In fact, ownership of real estate is legally described in terms of these rights or interests, and not in terms of what is owned.

> **Mnemonic = UPTEE**
>
> Use: The right to use of property, within the law in any way, or for any purpose
>
> Possess: The right to live on the property and the right to keep others out
>
> Transfer: The right to sell property, to give it as a gift, or to dispose of it in any way permitted by law
>
> Encumber: The right to borrow money and use property as security for the loan
>
> Enjoy: The right to peace and **quiet enjoyment** without aggravation by others

PROPERTY

Anything that may be owned and gained lawfully is known as **property**. Property can be real or personal. Anything that is not real property is personal property.

Feudal & Allodial Rights

Feudal - system of land ownership wherein all property was owned by the current monarch or an appointed noble.

Allodial - system of private land ownership in which individuals have the right to own real property.

Real Property

Real property includes the land, anything permanently attached to the land, anything appurtenant to the land, or anything immovable by law.

Real property is usually transferred by deed, devise, or descent.

Land

Land includes airspace, surface rights, subsurface rights, and water rights.

Airspace is considered real property to a reasonable height. An owner or developer of high-rise condominiums may sell the airspace as real property.

Surface rights are the rights to use the surface of land, including the right to drill or mine through the surface when subsurface rights are involved.

Subsurface rights are the rights to the natural resources (minerals, oil, and gas) below the surface. Saleable underground rights include oil and gas rights and mineral rights.

Certain water rights are considered real property because they are considered part of the land.

The owner of property bordering a river or stream has riparian rights. Owners of land bordering closed bodies of water, such as lakes or oceans have littoral rights and generally own the land up to the mean vegetation line.

Attachments

Attachments are items permanently attached to the land are real property and belong to the owner. These items include improvements, fixtures, and natural attachments.

Improvements

Improvements such as houses, fences, swimming pools, or anything resting on the land are permanent and owned as a part of the property.

Fixtures

A fixture is real property that used to be personal property. The tests to determine a fixture are adaptation and agreement of the parties, intent of the parties, and method of attachment.

> **Mnemonic = AIM**
> Adaptation of the Item & Agreement of the Parties
> Intent
> Method of attachment

Exception - Trade Fixtures

Trade fixtures are items of personal property used to conduct a business, such as shelves, cash registers, room partitions, or wall mirrors. Tenants are responsible for repairing any damage that results from removing the trade fixtures.

Growing Things

Natural attachments (growing things) are growing plants attached by their roots, such as trees, shrubs, and flowers. The two types of natural attachments are *fructus naturales* and *fructus industriales*.

Fructus naturales are naturally occurring plant growth, such as grasses, trees, and shrubs and are considered part of the real property.

Fructus industriales are annual crops produced by human labor, such as fruits, nuts, vegetables, and grains. **Emblements**, a specific type of *fructus industriales*, are annual crops cultivated by tenant farmers and sharecroppers. The crops are the personal property of the farmer who has a license to enter the land to care for and harvest the crop.

Personal Property

Personal property is everything other than real property and is often referred to as movable property, **personalty,** or **chattel**. Personal property can be transferred or sold using a bill of sale and may be pledged as security for a loan.

TYPES OF ESTATES

An **estate** is the ownership interest or claim a person has in real property.

Freehold Estates

A **freehold estate** is an estate of indefinite duration. The types of freehold estates are estates in fee and life estates.

Estates in Fee

Fee simple estate or **fee simple absolute** is the most complete form of ownership. A **defeasible fee** is a conditional estate.

Life Estates

A **life estate** is one that is limited in duration of a measuring life. The **measuring life** is usually the grantee's life—but it does not have to be.

It can even be created on the life of a designated person who has no interest in the property as the measuring life—known as **pur autre vie**, meaning for another's life. The holder of the life estate is called the **life tenant**.

Legal Life Estates

Some states have legal life estates. **Curtesy** is the husband's life estate in all, inheritable real estate of deceased wife. **Dower** is the wife's life estate in all, inheritable real estate of deceased husband.

Homestead

Many states have homestead laws to protect individuals and families against foreclosure from creditors. **Homestead** is a tract of land owned and occupied as the family home.

Less-Than-Freehold Estates

The **less-than-freehold estate** (also called a **nonfreehold estate** or a **leasehold estate**) is a tenant's possessory estate in land or premises. A leasehold interest in real estate and its duration is known as a **tenancy**.

Types of Leasehold Estates

An **estate for years (tenancy for years)** is for a fixed term and definite end date.

A **periodic tenancy (estate from period-to-period)** is a leasehold interest that is for an indefinite period—usually month to month.

A **tenancy at will** is created when a tenant obtains possession of the property with the owner's permission, but without a rental agreement.

A **tenancy at sufferance** (also called **holdover tenancy**) occurs when the tenant remains in possession after the lease expires.

The possessory right to occupy the property granted by the **lease** is personal property.

Upon a sale, an existing lease remains binding on the new owner.

Note: In the case of foreclosure, the foreclosing creditor's lien usually is senior to the tenant's right to possession under the lease, so most renters lost their leases upon foreclosure. However, since passing Protecting Tenants at Foreclosure Act of 2009 (PTFA), tenants are not promptly evicted following foreclosures. The PTFA allows tenants to stay until the end of their lease and month-to-month renters are entitled to 90 days' notice before having to move out. The PTFA expired in 2014.

OWNERSHIP OF REAL PROPERTY

Separate ownership and concurrent ownership are the two ways a person or other entity can take title to or own real estate.

Separate Ownership

Property owned by one person or entity is known as sole ownership, separate ownership, or **ownership in severalty**.

Individual
- Single man / single woman
- Unmarried man / unmarried woman
- Married man / married woman
- Widow / widower

Entity
- Individual
- Corporation
- Unit of government
- Limited Liability Corporation (LLC)/ Limited Liability Partnership (LLP)

Co-Ownership

Property owned by two or more persons or entities at the same time is known as **concurrent ownership** or **co-ownership**. The title is held jointly and severally.

Types of Concurrent Ownership
- Tenancy in Common
- Joint Tenancy
- Community Property
- Tenancy by the Entirety

Tenancy in Common

A **tenancy in common** consists of two or more persons, whose interests are not necessarily equal, with no right of survivorship. In most states, when two or more people purchase property they are tenants in common by default.

Joint Tenancy

Joint tenancy exists when two or more parties own real property as co-owners with equal interest and the right of survivorship. The **right of survivorship** means that if one of the co-tenants dies, the surviving tenant(s) automatically becomes sole owner of the property. There is no need for probate proceedings and the title passes immediately upon death.

In order to have a joint tenancy, the four unities—time, title, interest, and possession—must exist. If any one of the unities is missing, a tenancy in common is created.

The Four Unities of Joint Tenancy Mnemonic = TTIP	
Title	All parties must take title on the same deed.
Time	All parties must become joint tenants at the same time.
Interest	All parties must have equal undivided interest in the property.
Possession	All parties have equal right of possession.

Community Property

Community property is all property acquired during a marriage with the exception of separate property and property acquired by gift or inheritances. Nine states—Arizona, California, Idaho, Louisiana, Nevada, New Mexico, Texas, Washington, and Wisconsin—use the community property system to determine the interest of a husband and wife in property acquired during marriage.

Tenancy by the Entirety

Tenancy by the entirety is ownership by husband and wife in which each owns the entire property. In event of death of one, the survivor owns the property without probate (right of survivorship). Both spouses have an equal, undivided interest in the whole property.

Recording Ownership

Recording allows (rather than requires) documents that affect title to real property to be filed. A deed must be acknowledged to be recorded.

Acknowledgement is a formal declaration before a notary public or certain public officials, by the person (grantor) who signed (executed) the instrument (deed) that he or she in fact did execute (sign) the document.

Constructive notice is given to the world by recording the document.

Actual notice occurs if a person has direct, express information about the ownership interest of a property.

Priority means the order in which deeds and other instruments are recorded.

CHAPTER 1 – REVIEW

Multiple-Choice Questions

1. The term "property" refers to:
   a. the rights or interests in the thing owned.
   b. a freehold estate.
   c. personal property only.
   d. land and buildings only.

2. Which of the following is considered real property?
   a. Lumber
   b. Airspace above the land
   c. Unharvested crops under a prior sales contract
   d. Landfill soil being hauled

3. Which of the following is considered personal property?
   a. Mineral rights
   b. Leasehold estates
   c. All improvements to land
   d. Trees growing in a natural forest

4. Which of the following is considered personal property?
   a. Improvements
   b. Apple trees
   c. Emblements
   d. Trees growing in a natural forest

5. The highest quality and quantity of ownership in real property is:
   a. determinable fee.
   b. allodial ownership.
   c. life estate.
   d. fee simple.

6. Which test is not a general test of a fixture?
   a. Method of attachment
   b. Time of attachment
   c. Adaptability of the item
   d. Intention of the parties

7. Which of the following is a less-than-freehold estate?
   a. Life estate
   b. Estate of inheritance
   c. Estate for years
   d. Estate in remainder

8. An uncle left his nephew 2/3 interest and left his nephew's wife 1/3 interest in real property jointly and without the right of survivorship. The nephew and his wife will assume title to an estate that is classified as:
    a. community property.
    b. joint tenancy.
    c. tenancy in common.
    d. sole ownership.

9. Ownership in severalty would most likely involve:
    a. a fee simple defeasible estate.
    b. tenancy in common.
    c. ownership with other parties.
    d. sole ownership.

10. The words "time, title, interest, and possession" are most closely related to the concept of:
    a. severalty.
    b. survivorship.
    c. sole ownership.
    d. joint tenancy.

11. Which of the following would not be classified as personal property or a chattel?
    a. Airspace in a condominium unit
    b. An apartment lease
    c. Trade fixtures in a retail store
    d. A promissory note

12. If a landowner deeds land to a hospital but specifies that it may only be used for a hospital, this would be a:
    a. leasehold estate.
    b. homestead.
    c. life estate.
    d. defeasible estate.

13. The title to chattels, personalty, and personal property is transferred by a:
    a. mortgage.
    b. deed.
    c. deed of trust.
    d. bill of sale.

14. Concerning real property, in which way are joint tenancy interest and community property similar?
    a. Ownership interests are equal.
    b. Only a husband and wife are involved.
    c. Both owners must join in any conveyance.
    d. Neither provides for a right of survivorship.

15. Kris, Dan, and Alex took title to a property as joint tenants. Kris sold her share to Pat, and then Dan died. Who owns the property?

    a.   Alex owns 2/3 and Pat owns 1/3 as joint tenants.

    b.   Alex, Pat, and Dan's heirs own the property 1/3 each as joint tenants.

    c.   Alex owns 2/3 and Pat owns 1/3 as tenants in common.

    d.   Alex, Pat, and Dan's heirs own the property 1/3 each as tenants-in-common.

Answer Key

1. (a) Property refers to the bundle of rights or interests a person has in the thing owned.

2. (b) Land includes the surface and the space above and beneath for an indefinite distance and is included with land. Lumber, crops, and landfill soil are movable personal property.

3. (b) Mineral rights, improvements to land, and trees growing in a forest are real property. A leasehold estate, also known as a less-than-freehold estate, is personal property of the tenant.

4. (c) The fruit (apples) from orchards in a commercial grove and crops, which are grown and cultivated annually for sale, are called emblements. Emblements, or fructus industriales, are crops produced by human labor such as lettuce, grapes, fruits, nuts, wheat, corn, cotton, etc. Emblements are personal property, owned by tenants, as well as fee owners. Remember, the crops are the personal property, not the trees or plants on which they grow.

5. (d) Ownership in fee simple or fee simple absolute conveys the highest quantity and quality of ownership in the property.

6. (b) The tests to determine a fixture are adaptation and agreement of the parties, intention of the parties, and method of attachment.

7. (c) An estate for years is one of the four types of less-than-freehold estates. They are: (1) estate for years, (2) estate from period to period, (3) estate at will, and (4) estate at sufferance. Choices (a), (b), and (d) are freehold estates.

8. (c) It is not community property because the interests are unequal. Joint tenancy is impossible due to the unequal interest and lack of survivorship. Two or more owners cannot create a sole ownership. A tenancy in common would be created.

9. (d) Property owned by one person or entity is known as sole and separate, or ownership in severalty. Severalty means you are severed from other owners.

10. (d) The four unities of a joint tenancy are time, title, interest, and possession (TTIP). If formed properly, a joint tenancy creates a right of survivorship.

11. (a) When one purchases a condominium; they purchase a fee simple ownership in an air space, which is considered real property.

12. (d) The hospital's ownership is predicated on the condition that a hospital is built on the land.

13. (d) A bill of sale is used to transfer personal property.

14. (a) A joint tenancy requires equal interests. Community property ownership is also an equal 50/50 interest. Anyone may form a joint tenancy, so answer (b) is false. Answer (c) is true of community property, but one member of a joint tenancy may convey interest (and thereby dissolve the joint tenancy). Answer (d) is false because both forms of ownership provide for a right of survivorship depending upon the state's community property laws.

15. (c) A person may sell a joint tenancy interest, but may not will it. When Kris sold her interest to Pat, Pat became a tenant in common. Dan and Alex remained as joint tenants. When Dan died, Dan's third was automatically conveyed to Alex, who then became a tenant in common. Therefore, Alex ends up owning 2/3 and Pat 1/3—as tenants in common.

Chapter 2
Encumbrances & Transfer of Ownership

ENCUMBRANCES

An **encumbrance** is a non-possessory interest in real property that is held by someone who is not the owner. An encumbrance may create a **cloud on title**.

Encumbrances fall into two categories: those that affect the title, known as **money encumbrances (financial encumbrances)**, and those that affect the use of the property, known as non-money **encumbrances (non-financial encumbrances)**.

Money Encumbrances

A money encumbrance affects title and is a lien. A **lien** creates a legal obligation to pay.

Typical Money Encumbrances

- Deeds of Trust and Mortgages

- Mechanics' Liens

- Tax Liens. Property taxes, special assessments, or IRS tax liens

- Judgments

- Mortgage liens - created by the filing of a deed of trust

- M & M Liens - placed against a property by anyone who supplies labor, services, or materials used for improvements on real property

- Ad valorem tax liens - property taxes; the highest priority lien

Non-Money Encumbrances

A non-money encumbrance affects the use of property.

Typical Non-Money Encumbrances
- Building restrictions

- Easements

- Zoning requirements

- Encroachments

Deed restrictions, covenants, conditions and restrictions (CC&Rs), and zoning ordinances limit land use.

Restrictions

A **restriction** is a limitation placed on the use of property.

Deed restrictions and covenants are created in the deed at the time of sale or in the general plan of a subdivision by the developer.

Easements

An **easement** is the right to enter or use someone else's land for a specified purpose. An interest in an easement is non-possessory. The right to enter onto a property using an easement is called **ingress** (enter). The right to exit from a property using an easement is called **egress** (exit).

Classification of Easements

Easements are classified as appurtenant easements and easements in gross.

An **EASEMENT APPURTENANT** creates an ingress and egress; attaches to the land. The owner whose land is being used is the one giving the easement and the land is the **servient tenement**. The person's land receiving the benefit of the easement is known as the **dominant tenement**. An easement appurtenant automatically goes with the sale of the dominant tenement.

An **EASEMENT IN GROSS** is an easement that is not appurtenant to any one parcel. Easements in gross only have a servient tenement (no dominant tenement). Typical easements in gross include oil and gas pipelines and public utilities. These easements are considered personal property, not an interest in land.

Creating Easements

EXPRESS GRANT. The servient tenement, or the giver of the easement, grants the easement by deed or express agreement.

EXPRESS RESERVATION. The seller of a parcel who owns adjoining land, reserves an easement or right-of-way over the former property.

NECESSITY. An easement by necessity is created when a single parcel is partitioned leaving one or more parcels completely landlocked with no access to a street.

PRESCRIPTION. An easement by prescription may be created by continuous, uninterrupted use, by a single party or a number of parties, for the statutory period.

Terminating Easements

FAILURE OF PURPOSE. An easement may be terminated if the purpose for creating the easement no longer exists.

ABANDONMENT. The obvious and intentional surrender of the easement.

MERGER. If the same person owns both the dominant and servient tenements, the easement is terminated.

EXPRESS RELEASE. The owner of the dominant tenement is the only one who can release an easement. A usual way would be to sign a quitclaim deed.

Requirements for Terminating an Easement
Mnemonic = FAME

Failure of purpose

Abandonment

Merger

Express release

License

Permission to use property for a specific purpose. Unlike an easement, a license to use may be revoked at any time.

Encroachments

Placing a permanent improvement (fence, wall, driveway, or roof) so that it extends over the lot line into adjoining property owned by another is known as an **encroachment**.

HOW TITLE TO REAL ESTATE IS ACQUIRED OR CONVEYED

Real property may be transferred (**alienated**) by private grant, public grant, public dedication, or operation of law (court action).

- Will
- Descent (Succession)
- Natural Forces
- Adverse Possession
- Transfer by Deed

Will

A **will** disposes of property after death.

> **Witnessed will** - usually prepared by an attorney and signed by the maker (testator) and two witnesses
>
> **Holographic will** - written in the maker's own handwriting, dated, and signed by the maker.

The maker may change a will by a **codicil**.

Devise - gift of real property by will

Bequest or **legacy** - gift of money or personal property by will

Intestate means dying without a will. A **testator** is a person who makes a will and is said to die **testate.**

Probate

Probate is a legal process to prove a will is valid. Probate proceedings are held to determine creditors' claims and beneficiaries' interests in an estate upon the owner's death.

Executor / executrix is the person named in the will to oversee its provisions. **Administrator / administratrix** will be appointed by the court to oversee the administration and distribution of the estate of a person who dies intestate.

Descent (Succession)

Every state has laws regarding descent and distribution. **Succession** is the legal transfer of a person's interests in real and personal property under the laws of descent and distribution. When a person inherits property as a result of someone dying without a will, it is called **intestate succession.**

Natural Forces

Accession is a process by which there is an addition to property by the efforts of man or natural forces.

The gradual build-up of soil, or **alluvium**, by natural causes on property bordering a river, lake, or ocean is called **accretion**.

Erosion is the gradual wearing away of land by natural processes. The sudden washing or tearing away of land by water action is known as **avulsion**.

Adverse Possession

Under the **adverse possession** statutes, one can acquire title to property by actual occupation, which is notorious, hostile, and continuous for the statutory period.

Transfer by Deed

A **deed** is a legal instrument used to transfer an interest in real property. The **grantor** is the person conveying the property, and the **grantee** is the person receiving the property. A deed transfers title to real property and must be in writing.

Elements of a Valid Deed
- Legally competent grantor
- Legal description (in some states)
- Consideration
- Words of conveyance
- Named grantee
- Signed by the grantor, delivered to and accepted by the grantee

Legally Competent

The grantor must be legally competent to convey the property.

- Sane, not mentally impaired or under the influence of drugs or alcohol
- 18 years old, or
  - Married
  - Divorced
  - Member of the armed forces
  - Emancipated

Legal Description of the Property

There are three common ways to describe property: metes and bounds description; lot, block, and tract system; and the Public Land Survey System.

- Metes and bounds description
- Reference to a recorded document (lot and block or a condominium declaration)
- Government survey system (**Public Land Survey System**)

Consideration

- Money

- Love and affection

Words of Conveyance

- Words of granting (**grant** or **convey**) must be included. This is called a **granting clause**.

- Intent to convey from one entity to another

Named Grantee

- The grantee must be identifiable.

Signed by Grantor and Delivered to Grantee

- The deed must be executed (signed) by the grantor.

- The deed must be delivered to and accepted by the grantee.

Habendum Clause

The **habendum clause** begins with the words "to have and to hold" and defines or limits the ownership interest of the grantee. The grantor can reserve mineral rights, create life or remainder estates, and create various types of conditional estates and defeasible fees. The habendum clause is typically used in a warranty deed. Grant deeds do not usually include the habendum clause.

Not Necessary for Valid Deed

- Acknowledgment

- Recording

- Competent grantee (such as, minor, felon or incompetent)

- Date

- Signature of grantee

- Seal or witnesses

Types of Deeds

Different states and local jurisdictions have differing requirements for the types of deeds that may be used when conveying real property interests, including differing requirements for the form and presentation of the deed.

The kinds of deeds commonly used to transfer ownership include warranty deeds, bargain and sale deeds, grant deeds, and quitclaim deeds. Warranty deeds are used all over the United States and are the most commonly used deed in Texas. Grant deeds are used in some states and are the most commonly used deed in California.

General Warranty Deed

A **general warranty deed** contains five covenants.

Implied Warranties of a General Warranty Deed

1. **Covenant of seizen**. The grantor is the rightful owner with the legal right to convey title to the grantee. The grantee may recover damages up to the full purchase price if broken.

2. **Covenant against encumbrances**. The grantor guarantees that the property is free from any undisclosed encumbrances. If breached, the grantee can sue for the cost to cure.

3. **Covenant of quiet enjoyment**. The grantor ensures that the property's title can stand up to third party claimants who take action to establish superior title. If the grantee's title does not withstand, he or she may sue for damages.

4. **Covenant of further assurance**. The grantor ensures delivery of any instrument required to remove clouds on the title.

5. **Covenant of warranty forever**. It guarantees the quality of the title against any future failure. If title does indeed fail, grantor is liable.

Special Warranty Deed

In a **special warranty deed**, the grantor only warrants the title to the property during the time of the grantor's ownership.

- Used in sales of foreclosed property by lenders
- Used in sales in which the relocation company has taken title
- Used in estate sales

Bargain and Sale Deed

A **bargain and sale deed** (deed without warranty) is simply a deed that does not contain any covenant of warranty, but does imply ownership by the grantor.

Grant Deed

A grant deed must have a **granting clause** as well as two **implied warranties** by the grantor.

Implied Warranties of a Grant Deed

1. Grantor has not already conveyed title,

2. Estate is free from encumbrances other than those disclosed by the grantor.

Quitclaim Deed

A **quitclaim deed** is one in which the grantor only conveys the right, title, and interest of the grantor.

- No warranties or covenants to the grantee

- Used to release any interest the grantor has or may have

- Sometimes called a release deed

- Used to clear a cloud on the title

Public Grant or Land Patent

A **public grant** is the transfer of title by the government to a private individual.

A **land patent** is the document used by the government to show the original transfer title to land to an individual.

Involuntary Alienation - Operation of Law

Sometimes property is transferred by the operation of law without the owner's consent. It is usually an involuntary transfer involving foreclosure or is the result of a judgment or some other lien against the title. There are situations in which courts establish legal title regardless of the desires of the record owners.

Foreclosure is the legal process used by a lender to seize property of a homeowner for breach of a deed of trust or mortgage.

Bankruptcy is the court proceeding to relieve a person's or company's financial insolvency.

Quiet title action is a court proceeding to clear a cloud on the title of real property.

Partition action is a court proceeding to settle a dispute between co-owners (joint tenants or tenants in common) about dividing their interests in real property.

Execution sale is a forced sale of property under a court order with the proceeds used to satisfy a money judgment.

Escheat is a legal process in which real and personal property reverts to the state because the deceased owner left no will and has no legal heirs. The state must wait a number of years before trying to claim the property.

Eminent domain is the power of the government to take private property for the public use after paying just compensation to the owner.

Condemnation is the process by which the government acquires private property for public use, under its right of eminent domain.

CHAPTER 2 – REVIEW

Multiple-Choice Questions

1. Which is the best definition of encumbrance?
    a. The degree, quantity, and extent of interest that a person has in real property
    b. A non-possessory interest in real property that is held by someone who is not the owner
    c. The use of property as security for a debt
    d. Any action regarding property, other than acquiring or transferring title

2. The form of encumbrance that makes specific property the security for the payment of a debt or discharge of an obligation is called a:
    a. reservation.
    b. fief.
    c. lien.
    d. quitclaim.

3. Private restrictions on land can be created by deed:
    a. only.
    b. or written agreement.
    c. or zoning ordinance.
    d. both (b) and (c)

4. An owner of a parcel of real property gave a neighbor a deed conveying an easement for ingress and egress. The easement was not specifically located in the deed. Under the circumstances, the neighbor's right to use the easement is:

    a. enforceable because the location of the easement does not need to be specified.

    b. enforceable only if the easement is an easement in gross.

    c. unenforceable because the location of the easement must be specified.

    d. unenforceable because easements are created only by written agreement.

5. Gary owns a ranch. Gary gave Sam, who owns no property, a non-revocable right to cross his property to fish in a stream. Sam has a(n):

    a. easement in gross.

    b. license.

    c. easement appurtenant.

    d. easement by prescription.

6. The personal, revocable, unassignable permission to use the property of another without a possessory interest in it is called a(n):

    a. license.

    b. easement.

    c. encroachment.

    d. option.

7. Alienation of title to real property most nearly means to:

    a. cloud the title.

    b. encumber the title.

    c. record a homestead.

    d. convey or transfer title and possession.

8. A person who dies intestate:

    a. requires probate of the will.

    b. will have the estate administered and distributed by a court automatically.

    c. may have an executor designated by the court for the estate.

    d. will have their property escheated to the state.

9. What term identifies a will written entirely in the handwriting of the testator?

    a. Self-witnessed will

    b. Codicil

    c. Self-proving will

    d. Holographic will

10. Real property transferred under the provisions of a will is called a:

    a. quitclaim.

    b. bequest.

    c. devise.

    d. codicil.

11. A deed to transfer real property must be _____ to be binding on a buyer and a seller.
    a. recorded
    b. delivered and accepted
    c. acknowledged
    d. all of the above

12. The clause in a deed which sets forth the extent of the grantee's interest in the property is called the _____ clause.
    a. reversion
    b. habendum
    c. surveyor's
    d. assessment

13. Effective delivery of a deed depends on:
    a. the intention of the grantor.
    b. recording the deed.
    c. knowledge of the deed's existence by the grantee.
    d. acknowledgement of the grantor's signature before a Notary Public.

14. Which of the following covenants is not in a General Warranty Deed?
    a. Covenant of further assurance
    b. Covenant of warranty forever
    c. Covenant of encumbrances
    d. Covenant of seizen

15. Which action is a quiet-title action?
    a. Court action to foreclose
    b. Court action in ejectment
    c. Police action to quiet a noisy neighbor
    d. Court action to remove a cloud on title

16. A farm owned by Alex Green was escheated to the state because:
    a. Alex died intestate with no heirs.
    b. the state acquired the land for a highway exchange under eminent domain.
    c. Alex died and had no heirs.
    d. Alex did not pay taxes for the statutorily defined time.

Answer Key

1. (b) An encumbrance is an interest in real property that is held by someone who is not the owner.

2. (c) An owner may choose to borrow money, using the property as security for the loan, creating a voluntary lien.

3. (b) Private restrictions are created in the deed at the time of sale or in the general plan of a subdivision by the developer.

4. (a) The existence of an easement is obvious and necessary at the time a property is conveyed, even though no mention of it is made in the deed.

5. (a) Since an unlocated easement is valid, it is possible to have an easement that is not appurtenant to any particular land. These easements are known as easements in gross.

6. (a) A license is a revocable permission to use that property that may not be transferred to anyone else.

7. (d) Real property may be transferred, or alienated—by private grant, public grant, public dedication, or operation of law (court action).

8. (b) The court will appoint an administrator and the decedent's property will be distributed according to the Laws of Descent and Distribution.

9. (d) A holographic will is written in the testator's own handwriting.

10. (c) Real property inherited under the terms of a will is called a devise. Personal property is classed a legacy or bequest. A codicil is a change in the original will.

11. (b) Property is acquired by transfer when, by an act of the parties or law, title is conveyed, or transferred, from one person to another by means of a written document. A deed is binding when it is delivered and accepted.

12. (b) The habendum clause (the have and to hold clause) defines the extent of the estate being transferred.

13. (a) It must be the intention of the grantor that the deed is delivered and title be transferred during his or her lifetime.

14. (c) A General Warranty Deed has five covenants. They are the Covenant of seizen, the Covenant of quiet enjoyment, the Covenant of further assurance, the Covenant of warranty forever, and the Covenant against encumbrances.

15. (d) Quiet title action is a court proceeding to clear a cloud on the title of real property. It is frequently used to clear tax titles, titles based on adverse possession, and the seller's title under a forfeited, recorded land contract.

16. (a) If one dies intestate; his or her property will be escheated to the state after a prescribed period.

Chapter 3
Contracts: The Basics

A **contract** is an agreement made by competent parties to do (**performance**) or not to do (**forbearance**) a certain act for the breach of which the law provides a remedy.

To be valid, all parties must mutually agree (**meeting of the minds**). One party must **offer** and another must **accept** unconditionally. An **acceptance** is an unqualified agreement to the terms of an offer. The offer must be definite and certain in its terms, and the agreement must be genuine or the contract may be voidable by one or both parties.

CONTRACT CLASSIFICATIONS

EXPRESS CONTRACT - the parties declare the terms and put their intentions in words, oral or written.

IMPLIED CONTRACT - agreement is shown by act and conduct rather than words

UNILATERAL CONTRACT - contract in which one party promises to perform before the other party is obligated to perform

BILATERAL CONTRACT - agreement in which each person promises to perform an act in exchange for another person's promise to perform

EXECUTORY CONTRACT - something remains to be performed by one or both parties

EXECUTED CONTRACT - all parties have performed completely

Legal Effect of a Contract

VOIDABLE CONTRACT - valid and enforceable on its face, but may be rejected by one or more of the parties

VOID CONTRACT - no contract at all or has no legal effect

UNENFORCEABLE CONTRACT - valid, but for some reason cannot be proved by one or both of the parties

VALID CONTRACT - binding and enforceable with all the basic elements required by law

Basic Elements of All Contracts

- Legally competent parties
- Mutual consent between the parties (meeting of the minds)
- Lawful objective
- Sufficient consideration

As required by the statute of frauds, a real estate contract must be in writing to be enforeceable in a court of law.

Parol Evidence Rule

When two parties make oral promises to each other, and then write and sign a contract promising something different, the written contract will be considered the valid one. Parol means "oral," or by "word of mouth." The **parol evidence rule** extends this meaning and prohibits introducing any kind of outside evidence to vary or add to the terms of deeds, contracts or other writings once executed.

Under the parol evidence rule, when a contract is intended to be the parties' complete and final agreement, no further outside promises, oral or written, are allowed. Occasionally a contract is ambiguous or vague. Then the courts will allow use of prior agreements to clarify an existing disputed contract.

STATUTE OF FRAUDS

Most contracts required by law to be in writing fall under the Statute of Frauds. The **statute of frauds**, adopted in England in 1677, became part of English common law. With the exception of Louisiana, all states ultimately adopted some form of the Statute of Frauds.

The law provides that certain contracts are invalid unless they are in writing and signed by either the parties involved or their agents. By requiring certain contracts to be in writing, the existence and terms of these contracts is clarified for all concerned parties. The Statute of Frauds requires many types of contracts to be in writing.

All states seem to agree that two types of real estate contracts must be in writing.

Contracts that Must be in Writing.

(1) Sales (transfers and conveyances) of real property

(2) Any contract that takes more than one year to complete, such as a lease that runs for more than one year

DISCHARGE OF CONTRACTS

A **discharge of contract** is the cancellation or termination of a contract.

Ways to Discharge a Contract
- Full performance
- Release by one or all of the parties
- Assignment
- Novation
- Breach of contract

MUTUAL RESCISSION occurs when all parties to a contract agree to cancel the agreement.

An **ASSIGNMENT** transfers the interests of the assignor (principal) to the **assignee**.

A buyer may also purchase a property subject to the existing loan. A **SUBJECT TO CLAUSE** allows a buyer to take over a loan, making the payments without the knowledge or approval of the lender. The original borrower remains responsible for the loan, even though the buyer takes title and makes the payments.

A **NOVATION** is the substitution, by agreement, of a new obligation for an existing one, with the intent to extinguish the original contract.

A **BREACH OF CONTRACT** is a failure to perform on part or all of the terms and conditions of a contract. A breach of contract can result in unilateral rescission or a lawsuit.

- Unilateral rescission
- Lawsuit for money damages
  Liquidated damages (earnest money)

  Compensatory damages (determined by the court)

  Punitive damages (excess damages awarded adequately to compensate plaintiff for emotional distress)

  Exemplary damages (damages awarded for physical pain, mental anguish, or impairment of plaintiff)
- Lawsuit for specific performance

STATUTE OF LIMITATIONS

All states have some form of the **statute of limitations**. Any person seeking relief for a breach of contract must do so within the guidelines of the Statute of Limitations. This set of laws determines that civil actions start only within the time periods prescribed by law.

An **action** is a legal proceeding. Filing lawsuits within the allowed time prevents this right from expiring.

CHAPTER 3 – REVIEW

Multiple-Choice Questions

1. An agreement to do or not to do a certain thing is called:
   a. a contract.
   b. forbearance.
   c. mutual consent.
   d. negotiation.

2. When a promise is given by both parties with the expectation of performance by the other party, it is known as a(n) _____ contract.
   a. unilateral
   b. bilateral
   c. implied
   d. express

3. A 15-year-old individual may acquire title to real property by:
   a. payment.
   b. gift or inheritance.
   c. lawful object.
   d. proving adequate mental capacity.

4. The following elements are necessary to create a valid contract, except:
   a. consideration.
   b. acceptance.
   c. offer.
   d. performance.

5. Another name for mutual assent is:
   a. unilateral agreement.
   b. meeting of the minds.
   c. implied agreement.
   d. executory agreement.

6. Consideration is one of the necessary elements of a valid contract. Which of the following is consideration?
   a. A promise to perform an act
   b. An exchange of money
   c. A service rendered
   d. All of the above

7. All of the following are necessary for a valid contract, except:
   a. sufficient writing.
   b. genuine consent.
   c. lawful object.
   d. capable parties.

8. A written contract takes precedence over oral agreements. This principle is expressed by the:
   a. Statute of Limitations.
   b. Statute of Frauds.
   c. parol evidence rule.
   d. rule of previous evidence.

9. The statute of frauds requires that contracts for the sale of real estate must:
   a. be recorded.
   b. be in writing.
   c. be bilateral contracts.
   d. have a cash deposit.

10. A suit for specific performance is:
    a. a method of obtaining financing when the buyer falls a little short.
    b. a means of holding the seller to his/her promise to pay a commission.
    c. the way in which a seller can require the buyer to accept the terms of original contract.
    d. an option whereby the seller can require the buyer to meet the requirements of the earnest money contract and the buyer can require the seller to meet the terms of the agreed on contract.

Answer Key

1. (a) A contract is an agreement made by competent parties to perform or not perform a certain act.

2. (b) A bilateral contract is an agreement in which each person promises to perform an act in exchange for another person's promise to perform.

3. (b) Both minors and persons not legally competent may acquire title to real property by gift or inheritance.

4. (d) A valid, binding, and enforceable contract has all the basic elements required by law.

5. (b) Mutual consent (or mutual assent), is sometimes called a meeting of the minds.

6. (d) Generally, consideration is something of value such as a promise of future payment, money, property, or personal services.

7. (a) In order for a contract to be legally binding and enforceable, there are four requirements: (1) legally competent parties, (2) mutual consent between the parties, (3) lawful objective, and (4) sufficient consideration. In addition, a real estate contract must be in writing to be valid.

8. (c) The parol evidence rule extends this meaning and prohibits introducing any kind of outside evidence to vary or add to the terms of deeds, contracts, or other writings once executed.

9. (b) Real estate contracts must have all the elements of a valid contract. Additionally, according to the Statute of Frauds, real estate contracts must be in writing and must be signed by the parties.

10. (d) The sales contracts provide for a means for both the buyer and the seller to enforce the terms of the contract upon one party's default.

Chapter 4
Agency Relationships

This is a general discussion regarding agency relationships. Be sure to check your state-specific laws.

Common law agency gets its authority from the customs that originated from pre-colonial England and from the subsequent judgments and case law that have enforced and reaffirmed the customs.

Statutory law agency is drawn from the statutes and rules created by various legislative and governing bodies.

WHAT IS AGENCY?

Agency is a legal relationship also called a **fiduciary relationship** in which a principal authorizes an agent to act as the principal's representative when dealing with third parties.

A **principal** in a sales transaction is either the buyer or seller. The **agent** has the fiduciary duty of loyalty, integrity, and utmost care to the principal. This means that the agent bound by agency law acts in the best interests of the principal. There is an obligation always to act fairly and honestly with third parties. A **third party** is anyone the licensee is not legally obligated to provide with his or her advice, opinion, or loyalty.

Four Components of Agency
Mnemonic = CARD

Control of the agent by the principal

Acceptance of authority by the agent

Reliance on the agent by the principal (client)

Delegation of authority

Agency relationships between the public and licensees are best established by written contracts, which create a fiduciary relationship.

The agent works **for** the principal and **with** third parties.

A **power of attorney** is a written document that gives a person (known as an **attorney-in-fact**) legal authority to act on behalf of another person.

A **subagent** is a broker who accepts the offer of subagency offered by the listing agent and typically represents the seller with the buyer as a customer.

Subagent Chart
• Shows the buyer properties meeting the buyer's requirements and describes to the buyer a property's amenities, attributes, condition, and status • Completes a standard purchase contract by inserting the terms of the buyer's offer in the form's blanks and transmits all offers of the buyer to the seller on a timely basis • Informs the buyer about the availability of financing, legal service, inspection companies, title companies, or other related services

TYPES OF AGENCY RELATIONSHIPS

Single Agency   Broker represents either the seller or the buyer in a transaction.

Dual Agency   Broker represents both seller and buyer in a transaction. Broker must have mutual knowledge and written permission of the parties. It is **not permissible** in some states.

Buyer Agency   Broker represents the buyer through a written agreement.

Designated Broker   The broker appoints agents within his or her office to represent either the buyer or the seller. It is **not permissible** in some states.

Transactional Broker   The broker is not an agent of either party, rather the broker is a non-agent or facilitator. It is not permissible in some states. It is **not permissible** in some states.

CREATING AN AGENCY RELATIONSHIP

An agency relationship is typically created between an agent and principal by an **agreement,** but it may also be created by the actions of the parties. It is usually created by a **listing agreement** or **buyer representation agreement**.

Listing and Buyer Representation Agreements

Listing and **buyer representation agreements** are written bilateral (or unilateral) employment contracts by which a principal (seller or buyer) employs a broker to market or locate real estate for his or her client. It creates a **special agency relationship**. Depending on its wording, a listing or buyer representation agreement may be considered a bilateral or a unilateral contract.

These agreements are not standardized. To be enforceable, a listing agreement must be in writing.

Listing and buyer representation agreements designate licensees as **special agents** who are NOT granted the authority to bind the principal or client.

A **special agent** is employed to perform a specific task.

A general agent has the authority to bind the principal in a designated range of business matters.

A **universal agent** is authorized by the principal to act in virtually every situation that might occur in his or her client's life.

Types of Listing Agreements

Most states recognize the following types of listing agreements: exclusive right-to-sell listing, exclusive agency listing, and open listing.

Exclusive Right-To-Sell Listing

An **exclusive right-to-sell listing** is an exclusive contract in which the seller must pay the listing broker a commission if the property is sold within the time limit by the listing broker, any other broker, or even by the owner. It is a bilateral contract because both parties exchange promises to perform.

Exclusive Agency Listing

An **exclusive agency listing** is an exclusive contract in which the seller must pay the listing broker a commission if any broker sells the property. However, the seller has the right to sell the property without a broker, and pay no commission. Initially, it is a unilateral contract because nothing is owed unless the broker produces a buyer. It becomes a bilateral contract if and when the broker produces a buyer because at that point both parties have obligations that must be fulfilled and can be enforced.

Open Listing

An **open listing** is a listing agreement that gives any number of brokers the right to sell a property and earn the commission. An open listing agreement is a unilateral contract because only one party (the seller) is obligate to act if and when an agent produces a buyer.

Net Listing

A **net listing** can be any of the three previous listing types. It is actually a way to calculate the commission. The broker receives all the money from the sale of the property that is in excess of the selling price set by the seller. Usually, this type of commission arrangement is discouraged.

Buyer Representation Agreements

A **Buyer/Tenant Representation Agreement** gives the broker the exclusive right to represent the buyer or tenant in the purchase or lease of a property.

Terminating an Agency Relationship

At any time during the agency, the principal or agent may terminate the agency, except in an agency coupled with an interest.

Review - Termination of Agency Relationship

- Full performance
- Expiration of its term
- Agreement of the parties
- Acts of the parties
- Destruction of the property
- Death, incapacity, or insanity of the broker or principal
- Bankruptcy of the principal

CHAPTER 4 – REVIEW

Multiple-Choice Questions

1. Agents have a fiduciary duty to:
   a. all third parties.
   b. the general public.
   c. fellow agents.
   d. their principals.

2. Fiduciary refers to:
   a. sale of another's property by an authorized agent.
   b. duties owed the customer in a transaction.
   c. the collection of principles by which a broker must conduct his business.
   d. one who has the legal authority to act on behalf of another person.

3. The relationship in which a broker represents either the seller or the buyer in a transaction, but not both is called a _____ agency.
   a. transactional
   b. dual
   c. single
   d. designated

4. An agency can be created by:
   a. express contract.
   b. ratification.
   c. estoppel.
   d. all of the above.

5. An exclusive right to sell listing agreement is a(n):
    a. bilateral contract.
    b. promise for a promise.
    c. employment contract.
    d. all of the above.

6. An enforceable listing contract for the sale of real property must be:
    a. in writing.
    b. acknowledged.
    c. recorded.
    d. all of the above.

7. Broker Winters signed an exclusive agency listing to sell Baker's $365,000 house. Winters diligently advertised the sale of the house. One week before the listing was to expire; the house was sold through Baker's own efforts to a friend. Under current rules and regulations, Winters is most likely to receive:
    a. no commission.
    b. half of the commission.
    c. the costs of advertising the house.
    d. all of the commission.

8. In an exclusive agency listing, as a matter of law, the duration of the listing between the broker and seller is:
    a. whatever term is agreeable to both parties.
    b. three months.
    c. 90 days after the listing agreement is signed.
    d. not specified.

9. When the Seller signs the listing agreement, the Listing Broker represents:
    a. both the buyer and the seller in the transaction.
    b. the seller in the transaction.
    c. the buyer in the transaction.
    d. either the buyer or the seller as designated in the residential contract.

10. When the Buyer signs the Buyer Representation Agreement, the Broker represents:
    a. both the buyer and the seller in the transaction.
    b. the seller in the transaction.
    c. the buyer in the transaction.
    d. either the buyer or the seller as designated in the residential contract.

11. A real estate broker hired by the buyer to locate a property must comply with all of the following, except:
    a. the instructions of the buyer.
    b. the instructions of the seller.
    c. the law of agency.
    d. state licensing law.

12. An agency relationship may be terminated by all of the following, except:

    a. a fire destroying the property, which is the subject of the agency contract.

    b. the principal's refusal of an offer to purchase, which was presented in the name of a third party.

    c. mutual agreement of both the principal and the agent before the original term expires.

    d. the renunciation of the agency by the agent.

Answer Key

1. (d) Agents have the fiduciary duty of loyalty, integrity, and utmost care to principals.

2. (d) An agency relationship is a fiduciary relationship in which one person is authorized to act for another.

3. (c) In a single agency, the broker represents either the seller or the buyer in a transaction, but not both.

4. (d) An agency relationship is created between an agent and principal, by agreement, ratification, or estoppel.

5. (d) An exclusive right to sell listing agreement is a bilateral employment contract between an owner of real property and an agent who is authorized to obtain a buyer.

6. (a) The listing agreement is a written contract by which a principal, or seller, employs a broker to sell real estate.

7. (a) An exclusive agency listing is an exclusive contract where the seller must pay the listing broker a commission if any broker sells the property. However, the seller has the right to sell the property without a broker, and pay no commission.

8. (a) The duration of the listing is decided between the broker and owner. Every listing must specify a definite termination date.

9. (b) In the listing agreement, the seller authorizes the listing broker to be their agent.

10. (c) In the Buyer Representation Agreement, the buyer authorizes the buyer's broker to be their agent.

11. (b) The real estate broker is working for the buyer and hence would not follow the instruction of the seller.

12. (b) At any time during the agency, the principal or agent may terminate the agency, except in an agency coupled with an interest. An agency is also terminated by the expiration of its term, the full performance of the terms of the agency, the destruction of the property, or the death or incapacity of either principal or agent.

Chapter 5
Real Estate Contracts

CONTRACTS TO SELL/PURCHASE REAL ESTATE

According to the **statute of frauds**, a contract to purchase or sell real estate must be in writing to be enforceable.

The sale contract contains all the information that defines the offer and sale of the property.

Once the seller agrees to the offer and the buyer is informed of the seller's acceptance without any changes, the sales contract becomes a legally binding contract.

Equitable title is the interest that the buyer has in a property once a contract has been signed and accepted.

The contract is considered **executory** until all the terms are completed and the transaction closes.

A **counteroffer** is a rejection of a previous offer combined with a new offer. There are three options for the offeree when in receipt of an offer: acceptance, rejection, or counteroffer. A counteroffer voids the initial offer.

Simultaneous **multiple offers** may be presented, countered, or rejected in any order.

A **time is of the essence clause** means that the time limits found in the contract must be met exactly.

Option

An **option contract** is a written, unilateral contract between the owner of real property and a prospective buyer, stating the right to purchase, a fixed price, and time frame.

An **option to terminate contract** allows a buyer the unrestricted right to terminate during the option period.

The **optionor** owns the property (seller, lessor). The **optionee** owns the right to purchase or lease (lessee) the property.

LEASES

A **lease** is a bilateral contract between an owner (**lessor** / landlord) and a renter (**lessee** / tenant) which gives the tenant a possessory right.

Tenancy is also defined as the interest of a person holding property by any right or title.

Reversionary right is the right of the landlord to reclaim the property at the end of the lease.

Usually, leases for longer than one year (1 year plus 1 day) must be in writing and signed by the parties, according to the statute of frauds.

Classifications of Leases

Leases are generally classified in one of three ways: (1) type of real estate, (2) length of term, or (3) method of payment.

Type of Real Estate

A **ground lease** is a lease for only the land.

A **proprietary lease** is used in co-op apartment buildings.

A **residential lease** is used for all residential property including single-family homes, duplexes, and multiple-family dwellings.

Length of Term

Leases based on length of time are short-term or long-term leases.

Method of Rent Payments

Leases are classified by consideration or the method of rent payments: gross, net, percentage, or index.

Gross lease: A gross lease is also called a flat, fixed, or straight lease. The tenant pays an agreed-upon sum as rent and the landlord pays any other expenses such as taxes, maintenance, or insurance.

Net lease: In a net lease, the tenant pays an agreed-upon sum as rent, plus certain agreed-upon expenses per month (i.e., taxes, insurance, and repairs).

Percentage lease: A percentage lease is a lease in which the tenant pays a percentage of gross monthly receipts in addition to a base rent. A **straight percentage lease** is a lease in which the tenant only pays a certain percentage amount of the gross sales (generally used with large anchor stores).

Index lease: Escalation clauses allowing rent adjustments in commercial leases are frequently tied to increases in the **Consumer Price Index** for Urban Wage Earners and Clerical Workers (CPI-W).

Transfer of Lease

If the lease does not prohibit it, a lessee may assign or sublease his or her interest in the property to another person.

An **assignment** is the transfer of the entire leasehold estate to a new person, called an **assignee**. The original lessee (**assignor**) steps out of primary responsibility for the lease and a new lessee (assignee) becomes responsible to the landlord for all the terms of the original rental agreement.

A **sublease** transfers possession of a leased property to a new person called the **sublessee**. The original tenant, who is now the **sublessor**, is still primarily liable for paying the rent to the owner. The sublessee is liable only to the sublessor. This type of lease is called a **sandwich lease**.

Termination of Lease

Termination of a Lease

- Expiration of the term
- Mutual agreement
- Violations of terms and conditions
- Destruction of the premises
- Eviction

A **sale of the property** during the term of the lease does not usually terminate the lease.

The legal remedy to evict or remove a tenant is called **suit for possession,** also known as **forcible entry and detainer** or **unlawful detainer action.**

CHAPTER 5 – REVIEW

Multiple-Choice Questions

1. What is the status of a contract during the period of time after a real estate sales contract is signed by both parties, but before title actually passes? The contract is:
    a. unilateral.
    b. voidable.
    c. executory.
    d. interim.

2. Buyer Baker presented an offer to seller Sam for the purchase of a 10-year-old home in a quiet neighborhood. Seller Sam made a counteroffer to buyer Baker. Under these circumstances, buyer Baker:
    a. is required to accept seller Sam's offer.
    b. does not have to accept the counteroffer, but is still obligated under his original offer.
    c. has no obligation under his original offer.
    d. is obligated to make a new offer to seller Sam, if the counteroffer is unacceptable.

3. Buyer Baker's agent presented an offer to purchase to seller Donna. Seller Donna was delighted because the offer met all of her terms. In order to accept the offer, what must seller Donna do?
    a. Make at least one counteroffer
    b. Sign and date the earnest money contract
    c. Both (a) and (b)
    d. Neither (a) nor (b)

4. Seller Kris listed a vacant lot with a broker at $111,400. Buyer Brown submitted an offer of $111,000 that was to expire in three days. The next day, Kris made a counteroffer of $111,200. When Brown did not respond within the three-day period, Kris signed an acceptance of Brown's $111,000 original offer and instructed the broker to deliver it to Brown. Brown told the broker that he had decided not to purchase the property, but Kris insisted they had a deal. Based on these circumstances, which contract do they have?
    a. Valid
    b. Void
    c. Invalid
    d. Enforceable

5. An agreement not to close an offer is known as a(n):
    a. novation.
    b. option.
    c. rescission.
    d. subrogation.

6. Seller Paul gives an option to buyer Green to purchase Paul's ranch. This option most clearly constitutes a(n):
    a. voluntary lien on Paul's ranch.
    b. offer to enter into a contract.
    c. fiduciary agreement.
    d. contract to keep an offer open.

7. Which statement is correct regarding an option contract to purchase real estate?
    a. The optionor is not obliged to sell the property.
    b. The option is a bilateral contract.
    c. The consideration must be money in excess of $100.00.
    d. The optionee is not obligated to purchase the property.

8. The term tenancy, as used in real estate law, is best described as:
    a. the landlord-tenant relationship.
    b. retention of rights as a remainderman.
    c. a lessor in a lease agreement.
    d. a mode or method of holding title to real property by a lessee or owner.

9. The right of a landlord to reclaim the property at the end of a lease is called:
    a. a proprietary clause.
    b. reversionary interest.
    c. an assignment.
    d. possession is 9/10 of the law.

10. If real property is subleased, what is the interest held by the sublessor commonly known as a(n):
    a. double lease.
    b. freehold lease.
    c. assignment.
    d. sandwich lease.

11. Which situation would terminate a lease?
    a. Eviction
    b. Destruction of the premises
    c. Mutual Agreement
    d. All of the above

12. A suit for possession proceeding (unlawful detainer action) is most often taken by a:
    a. beneficiary.
    b. trustee.
    c. lessor.
    d. grantee.

Answer Key

1. (c) Usually there are terms in the contract that must be met during the closing period; therefore, the contract is considered executory until all the terms are completed.

2. (c) Making a counteroffer rejects the original offer and puts a new offer on the table.

3. (b) To accept the offer, the seller only needs to sign and date the earnest money contract in the correct location.

4. (b) In a real estate transaction, a counteroffer is the rejection of an original purchase offer and the submission of a new and different offer. If a seller rejects the offer and submits a counteroffer, the original offer automatically terminates.

5. (b) An option is a contract to keep open for a determined time—an offer to purchase or lease real property.

6. (d) An option is a contract to keep open for a determined time—an offer to purchase or lease real property.

7. (d) The option does not bind the optionee to any performance—he or she does not have to exercise the option.

8. (d) Tenancy is an arrangement, by formal lease or informal agreement, in which the owner (landlord) allows another (tenant) to take exclusive possession of land in consideration for rent.

9. (b) A reversionary right is the right of the landlord to reclaim the property at the end of the lease.

10. (d) A sublease transfers possession of a leased property to a new person called the sublessee. The original tenant, who is now the sublessor, is still primarily liable for paying the rent to the owner. The sublessee is liable only to the sublessor. This type of lease is called a sandwich lease.

11. (d) Other ways to terminate a lease are destruction of the premises, breach of conditions by either lessor or lessee, or eviction.

12. (c) If the tenant defaults on the rent or refuses to give up the premises, the landlord may have to resort to the operation of law for removal. The legal remedy to remove a tenant is called suit for possession or unlawful detainer action.

Chapter 6
Disclosures in Real Estate

DISCLOSURE OF AGENCY RELATIONSHIP

Every state requires agents to discuss the various agency relationships with the sellers and buyers that are permitted. Any brokerage relationship formed must be disclosed to the parties in a transaction.

DISCLOSURES REQUIRED IN A REAL ESTATE TRANSFER

Caveat emptor, a Latin phrase meaning, **"let the buyer beware,"** puts buyers on notice to examine the property and buy it at their own risk. A property sold **"as is"** means the property is being sold exactly as it is found. No property may be sold "as is" without a complete disclosure of the defect, even though a broker might possess a disclaimer of liability for the defect. An "as is" clause does not relieve a seller from the responsibility to disclose all known material facts to the buyer.

Condition of Property

The use of property condition disclosure statements is widespread. In some states, it is a mandatory disclosure form.

Material fact: Any fact that may affect value, desirability, and intended use of the property.

Latent defect: Structural defect in a home that may be hidden from a buyer, but known by the seller.

Flood Zones

Sellers must disclose possible flooding of the property and flood insurance. Flood hazard boundary maps show **flood zones** that are prone to flooding within communities. Flood hazard boundary maps are also used in flood plain management and for flood insurance purposes.

The **Federal Emergency Management Agency (FEMA)** created these maps in conjunction with communities, and made them available on many county web pages.

Environmental Disclosures

Numerous federal, state, and local laws have been enacted to address the problems created by environmental hazards.

Typical Household Environmental Hazards

- **Asbestos**: A mineral fiber used in construction materials, which has been found to cause lung and stomach cancer.

- **Radon**: A colorless gas known to cause cancer. Radon can be detected with a spectrometer.

- **Lead**: A highly toxic metal that causes major health problems.

- **Formaldehyde**: A chemical organic compound found in building materials, which may be a carcinogen.

- **Hazardous waste**: Materials—chemicals, explosives, radioactive, biological—whose disposal is regulated by the Environmental Protection Agency (EPA). This is also called **toxic waste**.

- **Household hazardous waste**: Consumer products such as paints, cleaners, stains, varnishes, car batteries, motor oil, and pesticides that contain hazardous components.

Lead-Based Paint Hazards

This disclosure pertains to residential housing built before **1978** because lead-based paint was banned for residential use in that year. It applies to both sales and rentals.

Superfund

The Comprehensive Environmental Response Compensation and Liability Act (CERCLA) established the Superfund to clean up hazardous waste dumps and respond to spills.

Federal and state laws help to rejuvenate and clean up brownfields. A **brownfield** is an abandoned commercial or industrial site or under-utilized neighborhood where redevelopment is complicated by actual or perceived contamination.

An **underground storage tank (UST)** is a tank with at least 10% of its combined volume underground that is used to store petroleum and hazardous substances. A leaking underground storage tank (LUST) is an environmental problem.

Stigmatized Property

A **stigmatized property**, as defined by the National Association of REALTORS®, is "a property that has been psychologically impacted by an event which occurred, or was suspected to have occurred, on the property, such event being one that has no physical impact of any kind".

Interstate Land Sales Full Disclosure Act

This federal law regulates land sales where two or more states are involved. Currently, the Interstate Land Sales Full Disclosure Act (ISLA) is regulated by the Consumer Financial Protection Bureau (CFPB). Subdividers that have 25 or more lots in one state and want to sell them in another state must give each prospective buyer a property report. The **property report** discloses information about the property and the transaction.

DISCLOSURES IN FINANCING

Truth in Lending Act

The **Truth in Lending Act (TILA)**, Title I of the Consumer Credit Protection Act, is aimed at promoting the informed use of consumer credit by requiring disclosures about its terms and costs.

A lender offering adjustable rate residential mortgage loans must provide prospective borrowers with a copy of the "Consumer Handbook on Adjustable Rate Mortgages".

Under **Regulation Z (Reg. Z)**, a creditor must furnish certain disclosures to the consumer before a contract for a loan is made. Regulation Z implements the Federal Truth in Lending Act ([12 CFR §1026) and since July 21, 2011 is enforced by the Consumer Financial Protection Bureau.

It requires lenders to disclose the total finance charge expressed as an annual percentage rate **(APR)**. The Truth-in-Lending Act also established disclosure **standards for advertisements** that refer to certain credit terms. If the annual percentage rate (APR) is disclosed, no more disclosures are required.

If any **triggering terms** are used in advertising, full disclosure is required.

Reg. Z Triggering Terms
- Down payment
- Number of payments or terms
- The amount of the payment
- The finance charge

Real Estate Settlement Procedures Act

The **Real Estate Settlement Procedures Act (RESPA)** is a federal loan disclosure law that protects buyers or borrowers who obtain federally related loans. RESPA applies to all federally related, 1-4 units, residential mortgage loans. A **federally related loan** is one that is insured or guaranteed by the government.

Since the adoption of TRID Rule, most closed-end mortgage loans are exempt from the requirement to provide the Good Faith Estimate of Settlement Costs (GFE), the HUD-1 settlement statement (HUD-1), and the mortgage servicing disclosure statement. Instead, these loans are subject to the disclosure, timing, and other requirements under Regulation Z discussed previously in the Unit.

However, lenders providing home-equity lines of credit (HELOCs), reverse mortgages, and mortgages secured by a mobile home must continue to provide the disclosures. The **special information booklet** contains consumer information on various real estate settlement services. The **GFE** lists the charges the buyer is likely to pay at settlement and states whether or not the lender requires the buyer to use a particular settlement service.

Currently, the **Closing Disclosure** developed by the Consumer Financial Protection Bureau (CFPB) is the standard form used to itemize services and fees charged to the borrower by the lender when applying for a loan for the purpose of purchasing or refinancing real estate. For loans that require a Loan Estimate and that go to closing, lenders must provide BORROWERS with a Closing Disclosure at least 3 business days before consummation of the loan.

The lender must provide a **Mortgage Servicing Disclosure Statement**, which discloses to the borrower whether the lender intends to service the loan or transfer it to another lender.

RESPA Rules

- Prohibits undisclosed rebates or **kickbacks**

- Requires lenders to use the **Closing Disclosure** for loans that require a Loan Estimate and that go to closing

- Prohibits fee splitting

- Limits the amount of funds lenders can require to be escrowed for ad valorem taxes and property insurance

The lender has the final responsibility for the accuracy of the Closing Disclosure.

Equal Credit Opportunity Act

The **Equal Credit Opportunity Act** (ECOA) ensures that all consumers are given an equal chance to obtain credit. It prohibits discrimination in granting loans.

Protected Classes

- Color

- Race

- Religion

- National origin

- Sex

- Marital Status

- Age

- Persons receiving income from public assistance

The **Equal Credit Opportunity Act (ECOA)** requires the following disclosures.

- Informing applicants of the reasons for terminating or denying credit, if requested

- Informing holders of existing accounts of their rights to have credit history reported in both spouses' names

- Giving written notice of the requirement that the Act prohibits discrimination against credit applicants

Redlining is an illegal lending policy of denying real estate loans on properties in older, changing urban areas, usually with large minority populations.

Consumer loans carry a three-day right of rescission. Real estate loans do not have this three-day right of rescission.

CHAPTER 6 – REVIEW

Multiple-Choice Questions

1. If a seller includes an "as is" clause in a listing agreement, the:
    a. seller has no further obligation to the buyer.
    b. seller must still disclose material facts to a prospective buyer.
    c. broker will be responsible for any repairs.
    d. theory of caveat emptor applies.

2. A(n) _____ is any fact that may affect value, desirability, and intended use of the property.
    a. latent defect
    b. disclosure
    c. "as is" clause
    d. material fact

3. Tom's home has foundation damage that created cracks down the walls and in the floor. He did not want to repair the damage so he just covered the cracked walls with new wallpaper and fresh paint and had new carpet and flooring installed to make the home look move-in ready. Tom then listed the property with Broker Green, not mentioning any of the damage. Broker Green did not notice any obvious problems and marketed the home as move-in ready. Buyer Kelly bought the home and did not discover the damage until six months later. Under these circumstances, who would be liable?
    a. Kelly is liable because of his lack of inspection.
    b. Green is liable because he had a duty to disclose latent defects to the buyer.
    c. Tom is liable because he withheld material facts from Kelly and Green.
    d. No one is liable, according to the doctrine of caveat emptor.

4. Which of the following is not considered a household hazardous waste?
    a. Motor oil
    b. Pesticide
    c. Dishwashing soap
    d. Oil-based paint

5. Residential property built prior to 1978 requires the:
    a. seller to disclose known information regarding lead paint.
    b. landlord to disclose known information regarding lead paint.
    c. agent of the seller or buyer to disclose known information about lead paint.
    d. all of the above.

6. Seller Sam listed his newer ranch-style home built in 2002 with broker Ted. What must Sam do in regard to the lead based paint disclosure?
    a. Give the buyer the pamphlet, *Protect Your Family From Lead in Your Home*.
    b. Complete statements verifying completion of the disclosure requirements.
    c. Give the buyer a 10-day opportunity to test for lead.
    d. None of the above

7. A property that has been psychologically impacted is known as a(n):
   a. stigmatized property.
   b. brownfield.
   c. "as is" property.
   d. UST property.

8. Gary Green, an agent with Ready Realty, is writing a real estate advertisement for his new listing. Which of the following statements is legally permissible if no further information is given?
   a. Low monthly payment of five hundred dollars
   b. Three thousand dollars down payment
   c. Liberal terms available to qualified buyer
   d. Seller financing at 8% interest rate

9. Under RESPA, the buyer is entitled to receive the HUD-1 Settlement Statement _____ business days prior to closing.
   a. 4
   b. 3
   c. 2
   d. 1

10. The Equal Credit Opportunity Act requires:

    a. giving written notice of the requirement that the Act prohibits discrimination against credit applicants.

    b. always informing applicants of the reasons for terminating or denying credit.

    c. informing holders of previous and existing accounts of their rights to have credit history reported in both spouse's names.

    d. all of the above.

Answer Key

1. (b) An "as is" clause does not relieve a seller from the responsibility to disclose all known material facts to the buyer. However, an "as is" clause indicates that the seller will not be responsible for the cost of repairing any defect.

2. (d) Any fact that may affect value, desirability, and intended use of the property is a material fact.

3. (c) The damage to the foundation, floors, and walls are latent defects, which should be disclosed to the buyer by the seller.

4. (c) Household hazardous waste include consumer products such as paints, cleaners, stains, varnishes, car batteries, motor oil, and pesticides that contain hazardous components.

5. (d) With properties built before 1978, whether purchased or rented, the seller and agents involved are required to present the buyer/tenant with information on lead based paint.

6. (d) This disclosure pertains to residential housing built before 1978 because the Act banned lead-based paint for residential use in that year.

7. (a) A stigmatized property, as defined by the National Association of REALTORS®, is "a property that has been psychologically impacted by an event which occurred, or was suspected to have occurred, on the property, such event being one that has no physical impact of any kind".

8. (c) Regulation Z requires full disclosure of all financial terms if one of the triggering terms is used.

9. (d) RESPA regulations state one business day prior to closing.

10. (d) Disclosures that are required by the Equal Credit Opportunity Act (ECOA) include the following: informing applicants the reasons for terminating or denying credit, if requested, informing holders of existing accounts of their rights to have credit history reported in both spouses' names, and giving written notice of the requirement that the Act prohibits discrimination against credit applicants.

Chapter 7
Escrow & Closing

Closing is a term that describes the completion of a property transaction. In different areas of the country, it may be called settlement, settlement and transfer, closing title, or closing escrow.

CLOSING PROCEDURES

Closing the real estate transaction is the final step on the path that began with getting the listing. In the United States, there are two different methods for closing property transactions.

One, called **escrow**, uses a neutral third party (called an escrow officer) to coordinate the closing. During escrow, the seller and buyer rarely meet. Escrow is most popular in the western states.

The second, sometimes called **non-escrow**, is conducted by attorneys, and brings the selling and buying parties together to sign papers and exchange the money and title. This meeting is known as a face-to-face closing, a closing meeting, or a settlement meeting. It is most common in the eastern United States.

Whether using an escrow (primarily west of the Rocky Mountains) or a closing meeting, the **closing** or **settlement** process includes signing documents that transfer title of the property from the seller to the buyer and distribution of funds. Closing is also sometimes called **settlement** or **settlement and transfer**.

TITLE

The goal of title insurance companies is to insure marketable title or good and indefeasible title of the property.

A **marketable title** is a title that a reasonable person would accept as clear and free from likely challenge.

Good and indefeasible title is title that cannot be defeated, set aside, or made void by a superior claim.

Chain of title is the succession of conveyances of the title. It is the public record of prior transfers and encumbrances affecting the title of a parcel of land.

Proof of Title

An **abstract of title** is a written summary of all useful documents discovered in a title search.

Certificate of title - an opinion of the ownership of title prepared by an attorney without an abstract.

Title Insurance

The parties to the contract stipulate who will pay for the owner's policy of title insurance.

As a condition of sale, the seller may not require the homebuyer to use a particular title insurance company, either directly or indirectly.

Types of Title Insurance Policies

The **owner's title insurance policy** is insurance that protects the homeowner against loss resulting from any defects in the title or claims against a property that occurred before the policy was issued.

A **commitment of title insurance** (title commitment) is a title report made as a condition of the sales contract. The title commitment is not a policy of title insurance, but is only an offer to issue a policy of title insurance in the future for a specific fee. It shows encumbrances, liens, or any other items of record that might affect ownership. It is also used as the basis for the final title insurance policy.

The **lender's title insurance policy** benefits the lender and ensures that the loan is a valid first lien (or second) against the property.

LEGAL DESCRIPTIONS

In most states, the street address (informal reference) is not adequate for a deed. However, it is sufficient for a lease.

Methods of Legal Descriptions
- Metes and Bounds
- Reference to a recorded plat
- Rectangular Survey System

Metes and Bounds

A **metes and bounds** description of land delineates boundaries and measures distances between landmarks. Landmarks (trees, boulders, creeks, fences, etc.) are called **monuments**.

A **benchmark** is a survey mark made on a monument indicating a known location and elevation. It acts as a reference point (**datum**) for surveying. This method of legal description measures the dimensions of the property using distance and direction. Land that is irregular in shape or cannot be described using either of the two other methods may have a metes and bounds description.

Metes mean measurements in length (measured in feet) from one monument to another. **Bounds** refer to direction. The direction of the boundary lines are given in degrees (°), minutes ('), and seconds ("). Generally, you will recognize this type of description when you see it. A surveyor will measure the distances and establish the legal description.

A metes and bounds description starts at a well-marked **point of beginning** (POB). The description continues by following the boundaries of the land, measuring the distances between landmarks, and returning to the beginning of the survey. Sometimes this is referred to as the **terminus**.

Reference to a Recorded Plat

The **recorded plat** is a map based on a survey of a parcel of land indicating where roads and lots are located.

It is also called the recorded map system, lot and block system, subdivision system, or the lot, block, and tract system.

Rectangular Survey System

The **rectangular survey system** (U.S. Government Section and Township Survey) is known as the **Public Land Survey System** (PLSS). It uses imaginary lines to form a grid to locate land. North-south longitude lines, called **meridians**, and east-west latitude lines called **baselines**, intersect to form a starting point from which distances are measured.

Imaginary vertical lines, called **range lines**, were drawn every six miles east and west of the meridian, to form vertical columns called **ranges**. Imaginary **township lines** were drawn every six miles north and south of the baseline to horizontal rows or **tiers of townships**. These rows were numbered according to their distance from the baseline. Thus, a grid of squares, called **townships**—each six miles by six miles (36 square miles)—appears. Each township is divided into 36 **sections** of 640 acres each.

Most states use PLSS to subdivide and describe land in the United States. The states that do not use PLSS include Maine, New Hampshire, Vermont, New York, Massachusetts, Rhode Island, Connecticut, Pennsylvania, New Jersey, Delaware, Maryland, Virginia, West Virginia, North Carolina, South Carolina, Georgia, Kentucky, Tennessee, and Texas.

TAX ISSUES IN TRANSFERRING REAL PROPERTY

FIRPTA

The **Foreign Investment in Real Property Tax Act (FIRPTA)** provides that if the seller of real property is a foreign person, the buyer must withhold a tax equal to 15% of the gross sales price. The IRS allows two exceptions from this 15% tax.

Exceptions Effective February 16, 2016
- If the sales price is $300,000 or less, AND the property will be used by the buyer as a residence, there is no tax and no money is withheld.

- If the sales price is between $300,001 and $1,000,000, AND the property will be used by the buyer as a residence, then a reduced rate of 10% of the sales price is withheld and remitted to the IRS.

However, withholding funds generally is not required when the seller provides a proper certificate of non-foreign status at closing called the **Seller's Affidavit of Non-foreign Status** including a U.S. taxpayer identification number.

Additionally, the withholding obligation may be reduced or eliminated when a **"withholding certificate"** is obtained through the IRS saying arrangements have been made for the collection of or exemption from the tax.

Tax Benefits of Home Ownership

Tax deductions are a way a homeowner can limit tax liability.

Deductible expenses

- Interest

- Property taxes

Non-Deductible expenses

- Maintenance

- Depreciation

- Capital improvements

Depreciation is not deductible on Schedule A of the IRS 1040 form. Depreciation is only applicable to assets used in a trade or business.

Sale of the Principal Residence

Individuals are generally permitted to exclude up to $250,000 ($500,000 for homeowners who file jointly) of gain on the sale of their principal residence from taxable income. To qualify, the taxpayer must have owned and occupied the property as a principal residence for at least two years during the five years prior to the sale or exchange.

Corporate Taxation

C corporation - double taxation because profits are taxed at the corporate level and dividends are taxed at the shareholder level.

S corporation - profits taxed only once at the shareholder level providing an owner of an S-corporation a tax advantage.

CHAPTER 7 – REVIEW

Multiple-Choice Questions

1. The completion of a property transaction is described as:
   a. closing.
   b. settlement.
   c. escrow.
   d. all of the above.

2. Title that cannot be defeated, set aside, or made void by a superior claim is called:
   a. chain of title.
   b. abstract of title.
   c. title insurance.
   d. good and indefeasible title.

3. What is an abstract of title?
   a. A brief description of the subject property
   b. A summary of all facts regarding evidence of title
   c. A guarantee of the validity of the title to property
   d. An informal description of the vesting

4. A buyer who wishes to insure title to real property when it is purchased should get a(n):
   a. title insurance policy.
   b. guarantee of title.
   c. certificate of title.
   d. abstract of title.

5. A _____ is an offer to issue a policy of title insurance in the future for a specific fee.
   a. title commitment
   b. lender's title insurance policy
   c. abstract of title
   d. certificate of title

6. Which of the following is not a type of legal description?
   a. Metes and bounds
   b. Rectangular survey system
   c. Subdivision system
   d. Street address

7. Which system of land description employs a point of beginning and a terminus?
   a. Metes and bounds
   b. Rectangular survey system
   c. Subdivision system
   d. Lot, block, and tract system

8. Which system of land description employs meridians and baselines?
    a. Metes and bounds
    b. Rectangular survey system
    c. Subdivision system
    d. Lot, block, and tract system

9. On the sale of a principle residence, which expenses are deductible?
    a. Interest
    b. Property taxes
    c. Both (a) and (b)
    d. Neither (a) nor (b)

10. Which business entity would be subject to double taxation?
    a. Sole proprietorship
    b. C corporation
    c. S corporation
    d. Limited liability company

Answer Key

1. (d) Closing is a term that describes the completion of a property transaction. In different areas of the country, it may be called settlement, settlement and transfer, closing title, or closing escrow.

2. (d) Good and indefeasible title is title that cannot be defeated, set aside, or made void by a superior claim.

3. (b) An abstract of title is a written summary of all useful documents discovered in a title search.

4. (a) The owner's title insurance policy is insurance that protects the homeowner against loss resulting from any defects in the title or claims against a property that occurred before the policy was issued.

5. (a) The title commitment is not a policy of title insurance, but is only an offer to issue a policy of title insurance in the future for a specific fee.

6. (d) In most states, the street address is an informal reference; not a legal description.

7. (a) A metes and bounds description starts at a well-marked point of beginning (POB). The description continues by following the boundaries of the land, measuring the distances between landmarks, and returning to the beginning of the survey. Sometimes this is referred to as the terminus.

8. (b) The rectangular survey system is also known as the U.S. Government Section and Township Survey or the Public Land Survey System. It uses imaginary lines (meridians and baselines) to form a grid to locate land.

9. (c) Both interest and property taxes are deductible on the sale of a principle residence.

10. (b) C corporation has double taxation. Profits taxed at the corporate level; dividends taxed at the shareholder level.

Chapter 8
Real Estate Finance: Loans

PROMISSORY NOTES

A **promissory note** is an IOU, a promise to repay, and the evidence of the debt. It is a negotiable instrument.

Interest is the **rent paid** for the **use of money** (capital). **Usury** is charging an interest rate that is in excess of the state established legal limits.

> The interest charged on most real estate loans is **simple interest**—interest paid only on the principal owed.

> **Compound interest** is the interest computed on the principal and any unpaid accumulated interest.

> The **prime rate** is the rate charged by commercial banks to their most credit worthy customers.

> The **discount rate** is the rate charged by the Federal Reserve Bank to member banks.

Repayment Plans

The manner in which the loan is repaid is described in the terms of the promissory note. Some notes are interest only and some are amortized.

A loan that calls for the payment of interest only until the maturity date when the entire principal is due and payable is called an **interest only loan**. It is also called a **straight loan** or **term loan**.

Amortization is described as the liquidation of a financial obligation through regular installments of principal and interest.

A **partially amortized installment note** calls for regular, level payments on the principal and interest during the term of the loan. The last installment, called a **balloon payment**, is much larger than the other payments.

A **fully amortized note (level payment loan)** is a loan with a fixed interest rate and level payments for the life of the loan. Regular, periodic payments to include both interest and principal are made, which pay off the debt completely by the end of the term. This type of loan is **fully amortized** because the loan and interest are fully paid when the last payment is made. With **biweekly** payments, the borrower makes 26 payments (pays 13 months worth) and will pay less in interest because the loan term is shortened.

An **adjustable-rate mortgage** (ARM) is one in which the interest rate is tied to a movable economic index.

ARM Terms

Index	Economic indicator used to calculate interest-rate adjustments.
Qualifying Rate	Discounted initial interest rate, often a **teaser rate** that is below a fully indexed rate. The rate is usually selected to be competitive in the marketplace.
Margin	Number of percentage points the lender adds to the index rate to calculate the ARM interest rate at each adjustment.
Periodic Cap	Caps that limit the interest rate increase from one adjustment period to the next.
Lifetime Cap	Caps that limit the interest rate increase over the life of the loan.
Payment Cap	Caps that limit how much the monthly payment may change, either each time the payment changes or during the life of the mortgage. Payment caps may lead to **negative amortization**, because the unpaid interest is added to the principal of the loan.

SECURITY INSTRUMENTS

Collateral, or security, is property pledged or **hypothecated** by the borrower as security for a loan.

Common **security instruments—deed of trust, mortgage, and contract for deed**.

Deed of Trust

A **deed of trust** is a security instrument that conveys title of real property from a trustor to a trustee to hold as security for the beneficiary for payment of a debt.

The three parties to a deed of trust are the borrower (**grantor**), lender (**beneficiary**), and a neutral third party called a **trustee**.

Mortgage

A mortgage is a security instrument that hypothecates the borrower's property as collateral for a promissory note. There are two parties in a mortgage: a **mortgagor** (borrower) and a **mortgagee** (lender).

Upon final payment and on demand, the mortgagee signs a **satisfaction of mortgage** that the debt is satisfied.

States that view a mortgage as merely a lien against property are called **lien theory** states. Those states that recognize the lender as the owner of the property are called **title theory** states. In **intermediate theory states**, the lender can take possession of the mortgaged real estate on default.

Contract for Deed

The contract for deed is a type of seller financing. The **contract of sale** is a financing instrument with many names. It may be called an installment sales contract, a contract of sale, an agreement of sale, a conditional sales contract, a contract for deed, or a land sales contract.

The seller (**vendor**) becomes the lender to the buyer (**vendee**) within this contract.

DEFAULT AND FORECLOSURE

Default is the nonperformance of a contractual obligation. A borrower who defaults on payments has the **right to reinstate** the loan and even forestall a foreclosure. The mortgagor (borrower) must bring the loan current as well as pay for all the expenses incurred by the mortgagee to foreclose the mortgage.

Foreclosure is the legal procedure used by lenders to terminate all rights, title, and interest of the mortgagor in real property by selling the property and using the sale proceeds to satisfy the liens of creditors.

Usually the lender will use a **non-judicial foreclosure** to foreclose using the **power of sale clause** in the deed of trust (with proper statutory notification), because it is the quickest and easiest method. Default on a mortgage, unless the mortgage includes a power-of-sale clause, requires a **judicial foreclosure**.

If during the foreclosure process, the borrower is able to satisfy the loan in full, including court costs and any interest, he or she may redeem the property. This is called **equity of redemption**. Selling the property at a foreclosure sale ends the borrower's right of equity of redemption.

A **deficiency judgment** is a personal judgment against a borrower for the balance of a debt owed when the security for the loan is not sufficient to pay the debt.

TERMS FOUND IN FINANCE INSTRUMENTS

An **acceleration clause** allows a lender to call the entire note due, on occurrence of a specific event such as default in payment, taxes, or insurance, or sale of the property.

The **alienation** or **due-on-sale clause** allows the lender to call the entire note due if the original borrower transfers (alienates) ownership of the property to someone else.

A **prepayment clause** invokes a financial penalty for the borrower that pays off a loan early.

An **assumption clause** allows a buyer to assume responsibility for the full payment of the loan with the lender's knowledge and consent.

The original borrower (seller) can avoid any responsibility for the loan by asking the lender for a **substitution of liability (novation)**, relieving the seller of all liability for repayment of the loan.

A **subordination clause** is used to change the priority of a financial instrument.

In a **Deed in Lieu of Foreclosure**, the borrower deeds the property whose loan is in default to the lender in return for the lender forgoing foreclosure.

CONVENTIONAL LOANS

A **conventional loan** is any loan made by lenders without any governmental guarantees. **Private mortgage insurance (PMI)** is required on loans with loan to value (**LTV**) in excess of 80%. It protects the lender in the event borrowers default on loans.

Conforming loans have terms and conditions that follow the guidelines set forth by Fannie Mae and Freddie Mac.

Non-conforming loans do not meet Fannie Mae/Freddie Mac guidelines for one of three reasons.

- The property does not physically qualify.
- The loan is in excess of the Fannie Mae/Freddie Mac loan limits for the current year.
- The borrower's credit does not qualify.

Loans that exceed the maximum loan limit set by Fannie Mae and Freddie Mac are called **jumbo loans**.

Subprime loans are loans less than "A" grade, such as "B" and "C" paper loans.

GOVERNMENT-BACKED LOANS

The **Federal Housing Administration (FHA)** does not make loans; rather, it **insures** lenders against loss. The lender is protected, in case of foreclosure, by charging the borrower a fee for an insurance policy called **Mutual Mortgage Insurance (MMI)**.

The **Department of Veterans Affairs (VA)** does not make loans. It **guarantees** loans made by an approved institutional lender.

PRIORITY OF RECORDING

Priority is the order in which documents are recorded and is determined by the date and time stamped on the document.

First deed of trust or mortgage - lien recorded first against the property

Junior lien - Any deed of trust or mortgage in a lower than 1st lien priority

A **subordination clause** is used to change the priority of a financial instrument. The lienholder voluntarily accepts a lower lien position than that to which he or she would normally be entitled.

TYPES OF LOAN PROGRAMS

Budget loan. The payment of principal, interest, property taxes, and hazard insurance (**PITI**) in one monthly payment.

Blanket loan. A deed of trust or mortgage that covers more than one parcel of property. It usually contains a **partial release clause** that provides for the release of any particular parcel upon the repayment of a specified part of the loan.

Package loan. A loan on both real and personal property. The borrower pledges both real and personal property (appliances) with a single security instrument. Often used for a furnished condominium.

Participation loan. A loan in which more than one lender owns a share.

Open-end loan. A revolving line of credit.

Swing loan (bridge loan). Temporary loan made on a borrower's equity in his or her home.

Equity is the difference between the value of the property and any outstanding loans or the initial down payment. Another type of swing loan is an **interim loan**. It is used to finance construction costs, such as the building of a new home.

Takeout loan is the permanent loan that pays off a construction loan.

Pledged account mortgage (PAM). Loan made against security, such as money held in a savings account or a certificate of deposit.

Shared appreciation mortgage (SAM). Loan in which the lender offers a below-market interest rate in return for a portion of the profits made by the homeowner when the property is sold.

Rollover mortgage (ROM). Loan in which the unpaid balance is refinanced typically every five years at then-current rates.

Wrap-around mortgage. Wraps an existing loan with a new loan, and the borrower makes one payment for both.

Reverse annuity mortgage. Program for homeowners who are 62 years or older. It allows homeowners to receive periodic payments from the lender based on the equity in their homes. The borrower is not required to make payments as long as the borrower lives in the home. The loan is due upon the death of the borrower or when the property is sold.

Home Equity Line of Credit

A **home equity line of credit (HELOC)** is a type of revolving credit in which a borrower's home serves as the collateral.

It has a low starting interest rate, with a variable monthly rate based on outstanding balance.

Home equity plans use variable interest rates based on a publicly available index, such as the prime rate published in some major daily newspapers or a U.S. Treasury bill rate. The interest rate will change, mirroring fluctuations in the index. To figure the interest rate that the borrower will pay, most lenders add a margin of one or two percentage points to the index value.

CHAPTER 8 – REVIEW

Multiple-Choice Questions

1. A promissory note:
   - a. is security for a deed of trust.
   - b. is evidence of a debt.
   - c. must be recorded.
   - d. is collateral for the loan.

2. All of the following are negotiable instruments, except a(n):
   - a. personal check.
   - b. promissory note.
   - c. installment note.
   - d. deed of trust securing a promissory note.

3. The liquidation of financial obligation on an installment basis is known as:
   - a. conversion.
   - b. acceleration.
   - c. conveyance.
   - d. amortization.

4. Which loan involves a balloon payment?
   - a. Fully amortized loan
   - b. Partially amortized loan
   - c. Variable rate loan
   - d. Fixed rate loan

5. When compared to a 25-year amortized loan, a 30-year amortized loan has:
   - a. higher monthly payments of principal.
   - b. higher monthly payments of principal and interest.
   - c. lower monthly payments of principal.
   - d. lower monthly payments of principal and interest.

6. A mortgage loan with an interest rate that changes along with money market rates is often referred to as a:
   - a. growing equity.
   - b. shared appreciation.
   - c. adjustable rate.
   - d. reverse annuity.

7. Which statement best describes a mortgage loan?
   - a. A loan secured by a mortgage on real estate
   - b. Any means of creating a trusteeship
   - c. An unsecured loan in which the mortgage itself serves as collateral
   - d. None of the above

8. A power of sale or trustee's sale foreclosure of a deed of trust:
    a. is similar to a court foreclosure.
    b. is faster than a judicial foreclosure.
    c. allows for no reinstatement period.
    d. gives the trustor rights of redemption.

9. Mortgages and deed of trusts are different in all of the following ways, except:
    a. parties.
    b. security.
    c. foreclosure.
    d. title.

10. In the case of a contract of sale, the best analogy for the financial relationship of the parties is:
    a. landlord-tenant.
    b. beneficiary-trustor.
    c. optionor-optionee.
    d. grantor-grantee.

11. Adding an acceleration clause to a note would:
    a. not make the note less negotiable.
    b. be of no benefit to the holder.
    c. make the note non-negotiable.
    d. greatly limit the negotiability of the note.

12. Buyer Gayle purchases a home from seller Sarah and agrees to assume an existing conventional loan. The lender agrees to the assumption and signs a substitution of liability. Under these circumstances:

    a. Gayle becomes primarily responsible for the loan, and Sarah remains liable as a surety.

    b. Sarah remains primarily responsible for the loan, and Gayle becomes secondarily liable.

    c. Sarah is relieved from all liability.

    d. the loan may not be secured by a purchase-money deed of trust.

13. The FHA was established to:
    a. help stabilize the housing market.
    b. promote home ownership by insuring home loans.
    c. raise building standards on a national basis.
    d. provide a source of home-loan funds at low rates.

14. A deed of trust and note are given to a seller to finance the purchase of vacant land. The buyer intends to place a short-term construction loan on the land. Such a deed of trust is most likely to include a(n) _____ clause.
    a. subrogation
    b. or more
    c. subordination
    d. prepayment

15. Fred borrowed money from Tim. As security for the loan, Fred gave Tim a deed of trust covering six separate parcels of previously unencumbered real property that Fred owned. This is an example of a(n) _____ loan.
    a. blanket
    b. subordinated
    c. all-inclusive
    d. purchase-money

Answer Key

1. (b) The promissory note is the evidence of the debt.

2. (d) A deed of trust is not negotiable but the promissory note is. The most common type of negotiable instrument is an ordinary bank check.

3. (d) Amortization is described as the liquidation of a financial obligation. It is the paying off of a loan (interest and principal) by the end of the loan's term.

4. (b) The partially amortized installment note calls for regular, level payments on the principal and interest during the term of the loan. Since the loan does not fully amortize over the original term, there is still a remaining principal loan balance. The last installment, called a balloon payment.

5. (d) Typically, the longer the term of the loan, the lower the monthly payment. However, the total financing costs over the life of the loan will be higher.

6. (c) An adjustable-rate mortgage (ARM) is one in which the interest rate is tied to a movable economic index. The interest rate in the note varies upward or downward over the term of the loan, depending on the agreed-upon index.

7. (a) The promissory note shows the obligation of the debt, and the mortgage is a lien against the described property until the debt is repaid.

8. (b) Non-judicial foreclosures take less time and cost less, so lenders usually prefer this method of foreclosure.

9. (b) In fact, the only thing deeds of trust and mortgages have in common is that the property is used as security for the debt.

10. (b) The vendor (seller) and vendee's (buyer's) relationship is like that of a lender (beneficiary) and a borrower (trustor) in a deed of trust.

11. (a) A promissory note is a negotiable instrument. A negotiable instrument is easily transferable from one person to another meaning it can be bought and sold. Promissory notes and deeds of trust may also include special clauses that give a general description of the duties and responsibilities of the trustor. The most common clauses are acceleration and alienation.

12. (c) The original borrower (seller) can avoid any responsibility for the loan by asking the lender for a substitution of liability (novation), relieving the seller of all liability for repayment of the loan.

13. (b) The FHA was established to improve the construction and financing of housing. The main purpose of the FHA program has been to promote home ownership.

14. (c) A subordination clause is used to change the priority of a financial instrument. This clause is used mainly when land is purchased for future purposes of construction that will require financing.

15. (a) A blanket loan that covers more than one parcel of property may be secured by a deed of trust.

Chapter 9
Real Estate Finance:
Lending Institutions

THE FEDERAL RESERVE SYSTEM

The **Federal Reserve Bank System** (the Fed) is the nation's central bank and acts as the banker's bank. The Fed's primary purpose is to regulate the flow of money and credit, and to promote economic growth with stability.

Ways the Fed Implements Monetary Policy

- Reserve requirements
- Discount rates
- Open market operations

THE MORTGAGE MARKETS

The residential mortgage market is made up of two markets: (1) the primary mortgage market and (2) the secondary mortgage market.

Primary Mortgage Market

The **primary mortgage market** is the market in which lenders make mortgage loans by lending directly to borrowers.

Savers deposit money in a financial intermediary, such as a bank, credit union, or brokerage firm, who then invest the money in stocks, bonds, mortgages, or government securities. This is called **intermediation**.

When savers withdraw their money from their savings accounts and put it into investments that pay a higher rate of interest, it is a process called **disintermediation**.

The lender may charge loan origination fees or discount points for making the loan. A **loan origination fee** is usually computed as a percentage of the loan amount. **Points** are a percentage of the loan amount paid to the lender when negotiating a loan. One point is equal to 1% of the loan amount. Points increase the lenders real yield by $1/8^{th}$ of 1% per point charged.

Most lenders sell the loans to participants in the secondary mortgage market.

Lenders in the Primary Mortgage Market

Commercial banks are the all-purpose lenders who make short-term home loans or interim loans to finance construction.

Thrifts, the largest single resource for residential mortgage credit, include savings and loan associations (S&Ls), savings banks, and mutual savings banks. **Mutual savings banks** are located primarily in the northeastern section of the United States. Deposits are insured by the Federal Deposit Insurance Corporation (FDIC). Currently, thrifts are the largest single resource for residential mortgage credit.

Credit unions provide loans to their members at rates lower than other lenders can offer.

Insurance companies are major suppliers of long-term money for large commercial loans. Loans made by insurance companies have low interest rates and the lowest loan-to-value ratio. Usually loans are made through loan correspondents (mortgage companies) who negotiate and service the loans.

Private individuals (sellers) are the major source of junior loans.

Mortgage bankers originate, fund, and often service their own loans and sometimes package those loans for sale to the secondary market. The process of assembling a number of mortgage loans into one package, prior to selling them to an investor, is called **warehousing**.

Mortgage brokers originate loans for other lenders, but do not service the loans.

Secondary Mortgage Market

The **secondary mortgage market** is for buying and selling existing mortgages acquired from the primary mortgage market.

Participants in the Secondary Market

The **Federal National Mortgage Association (Fannie Mae)** is a privately owned financial corporation who is the largest investor in the secondary market.

Government National Mortgage Association (Ginnie Mae) guarantees investors the timely payment of principal and interest on mortgage-backed securities backed by federally insured or guaranteed loans—mainly loans insured by FHA or guaranteed by the VA.

The **Federal Home Loan Mortgage Corporation (Freddie Mac)** is a stockholder-owned corporation charted by Congress in 1970 to stabilize the mortgage markets and support homeownership and affordable rental housing.

FINANCE TERMS

Credit scoring is an objective, statistical method that lenders use to assess the borrower's credit risk at a given point in time.

Credit rating is a representation of a person's creditworthiness based on their present condition and financial history.

Leverage is using borrowed money to finance property purchases.

Loan-to-value (LTV) is the percentage of the loan to the appraised value.

The difference between the appraised value of a property and the loan is called equity.

THE COMMUNITY REINVESTMENT ACT

The **Community Reinvestment Act (CRA)** encourages regulated financial institutions to serve their immediate community's needs.

Federally regulated financial institutions must:
- Define their community
- Make information available to the public
- Demonstrate that the institution is reinvesting in its community
- Meet the credit needs of the community

CHAPTER 9 – REVIEW

Multiple-Choice Questions

1. What is the largest single resource for residential mortgage credit?
   a. Commercial banks
   b. Credit unions
   c. Life insurance companies
   d. Thrifts

2. Which lender would loan the funds for construction costs for a single-family residence?
   a. Commercial bank
   b. Pension fund
   c. Savings and loan association
   d. Life insurance company

3. Which real estate lender has lending policies characterized by long-term financing, few construction loans, and a preference for larger loans that usually are not serviced?
   a. Commercial banks
   b. Mortgage companies
   c. Insurance companies
   d. Savings and loan associations

4. Life insurance companies usually do not deal directly with mortgagors or trustors. They make real estate mortgage loans through:
   a. the FHA or VA.
   b. mortgage companies.
   c. savings and loan associations.
   d. all of the above.

5. In the context of financing real property, the term warehousing most closely refers to:
   a. a large loan on a storage facility.
   b. a mortgage banker collecting loans before selling them.
   c. loans regulated by the Federal Reserve Board.
   d. underwriting stock issues with loans secured by industrial property.

6. Most junior loans negotiated in today's market are secured from:
   a. private lenders.
   b. commercial banks.
   c. private mortgage insurance companies.
   d. savings and loan associations.

7. In the field of real estate financing, the term secondary mortgage market usually refers to:
    a.   junior liens.
    b.   secondary financing.
    c.   unsecured financial instruments.
    d.   the resale or transfer of existing deed of trust loans.

8. The original purpose of the Federal National Mortgage Association (Fannie Mae) was:
    a.   buying and selling FHA-insured and VA-guaranteed loans in the secondary market.
    b.   buying and selling conventional loans in the secondary market.
    c.   buying FHA and VA loans in the primary market.
    d.   selling FHA and VA loans in the primary market.

9. Which of the following does not participate in the secondary market for mortgage loans?
    a.   Ginnie Mae
    b.   FHA
    c.   Fannie Mae
    d.   Freddie Mac

10. Which of the following charges would be used to increase the yield to a lender on a real estate loan?
    a.   Discount points
    b.   Appraisal fee
    c.   Title insurance
    d.   Origination fees

Answer Key

1. (d) Thrifts are the largest single resource for residential mortgage credit.

2. (a) The major type of lending activity funded by commercial banks is for short-term (6-to-36 months) construction loans, even though they do make other types of loans as well.

3. (c) Insurance companies are major suppliers of money for large commercial loans to developers and builders. Commercial real estate is a good, long-term investment for insurance companies because of the long time-line of their investment goals. They usually do not make construction loans, but make take out loans on large properties.

4. (b) Usually loans are made through loan correspondents (mortgage companies) who negotiate and service the loans.

5. (b) The process of assembling a number of mortgage loans into one package, prior to selling them to an investor, is called warehousing.

6. (a) Private individuals (sellers) are the major source of junior loans.

7. (d) The secondary mortgage market is for buying and selling existing mortgages from the primary mortgage market or from each other.

8. (a) The Federal National Mortgage Association (Fannie Mae) was originally created for the purpose of increasing the amount of housing credit available in the economy by purchasing FHA-insured and VA-guaranteed loans.

9. (b) There are three major participants in the secondary mortgage market: (1) the Federal National Mortgage Association, (2) the Government National Mortgage Association, and (3) the Federal Home Loan Mortgage Corporation.

10. (a) Discount points are used to increase the effective note rate or yield to the lender.

Chapter 10
Valuation & Appraisal

An **appraisal** is an unbiased estimate or opinion of the property value on a given date.

A **comparative (competitive) market analysis (CMA)** is created to identify the range of values for a particular property by identifying currently listed properties (the **competition**), recently sold and closed properties (the **successes**), and the expired listings (the **failures** or properties that did not sell on the market).

DEFINITION OF VALUE

Value is the present worth of rights to future benefits that come from property ownership.

Fair market value or market value is the price a property would bring if freely offered on the open market, with both a **willing buyer** and a **willing seller**. Multiple offers and a short market time indicate a **seller's market**. A **buyer's market** would have an **oversupply** of inventory.

Market price is the price at which the property changes hands between a willing buyer and seller.

Market value is sometimes called the **objective value**, since it may be determined by actual data.

Utility value is the usefulness of the property to its owner. This is **subjective value** or the value given for personal reasons.

Liquidation value is a likely price that a property would bring in a forced sale (foreclosure or tax sale).

Going concern value is the value of a company if sold as a continuing business rather than liquidated.

Four Elements to Create Value

The four elements of value that must be present for a property to have market value are demand, utility, scarcity, and transferability.

Mnemonic = DUST
    Demand

    Utility

    Scarcity

    Transferability

Forces Influencing Value

Value is created, maintained, modified, and destroyed by the relationship of four forces: physical characteristics, economic influences, political or governmental regulations, and social ideals.

Physical Characteristics

Physical characteristics are also called external characteristics. These characteristics include quality of conveniences such as availability of schools, shopping, public transportation, churches, and similarity of land use. **Location** may be the most important factor influencing value, as far as highest and best use. Another term used to describe where the physical location of property is **situs**. **Plottage increment** is the increased value of smaller, less-valuable parcels being combined under one ownership through the process of **assemblage**. **Environmental** forces may be climate, soil, topography, oceans, and mountains.

Economic Influences

Economic influences include natural resources, industrial and commercial trends, employment trends, availability of money and credit, interest rates, price levels, tax loads, economic base, new development, and rental and price patterns. A **blighted area** is a section of a city, generally the inner city, where most of the buildings are run-down and the property values are extremely low. **Inflation** is an unearned increment that affects property value. An **unearned increment** is an increase in real estate value that comes about from forces outside the control of the owner, such as a favorable shift in population.

Political Forces

Political forces include building codes, zoning laws, public health measures, fire regulations, rent controls, and pending legislation.

Social Ideals and Standards

Social ideals and **standards** include population growth and decline, age, marriage, birth, divorce, and death rates, which all combine to cause changes in social patterns. The study of population is called **demography**.

Mnemonic = PEPS

Physical characteristics

Economic influences

Political or governmental regulations

Social ideals

PRINCIPLES OF VALUATION

Valuation is the process of estimating market value for real property as of a specific time.

Principle of Highest and Best Use - Reasonable use of real property at the time of the appraisal, which is most likely to produce the greatest **net return** to the land and/or the building over a given period of time.

Principle of Supply and Demand - Increasing supply or decreasing demand will reduce the price in the market. Reducing supply or increasing demand will raise the price in the market. **Demand** is how much of a product is desired by buyers, whereas **supply** is how much of the product the market can offer.

Principle of Substitution - Value is set by the cost of getting an equally desirable substitute.

Principle of Anticipation - Probable future benefits to be derived from a property will increase the value.

Principle of Change - An appraiser must be aware of trends that affect the value of real estate.

Principle of Conformity - When land uses are compatible and homes are similar in design and size, the maximum value is realized.

Principle of Progression - A lesser-valued property will be worth more because of the presence of greater-valued properties nearby.

Principle of Regression - A greater-valued property will be worth less because of the presence of lower-valued properties nearby. An **overimprovement** is one that is not the highest and best use for the site on which it is placed by reason of excess size or cost.

Principle of Contribution - The worth of an improvement and what it adds to the entire property's market value, regardless of the actual cost of the improvement.

Principle of Balance - When contrasting, opposing, or interacting elements are in balance in a neighborhood or area, value is created.

APPRAISAL PROCESS

Professional appraisers have developed an orderly systematic method—known as the **appraisal process**—to arrive at an estimate of value.

Steps in the Appraisal Process

1. State the problem

2. Gather data (general and specific)

3. Decide on the appraisal approach to be used

   - Sales Comparison (Market) Approach
   - Cost Approach
   - Income Approach

4. Verify and reconcile the data

5. Arrive at a final value estimate

6. Write the report. Each written appraisal report must be prepared according to the Uniform Standards of Professional Appraisal Practice (USPAP) standards.

   Appraisal Report - Uniform Residential Appraisal Report (URAR) - most commonly used

   Restricted Appraisal Report - the use of the report is limited to the client

APPRAISAL APPROACHES

- Sales Comparison (Market) Approach
- Cost Approach
- Income Approach

Sales Comparison (Market Data) Approach

The sales comparison approach uses the principle of substitution to compare recent sales and listings of similar properties in the area.

Sales comparison approach is used primarily for residential properties.

Comparables are properties similar to the subject property that have sold within the previous six months.

Cost Approach

In the cost approach, land and improvements are valued separately.

Cost approach sets the upper limit of value.

Cost approach is used primarily for new buildings, special-purpose buildings, or properties with few or no comparables.

Cost approach takes the reproduction or replacement cost of the improvements minus accrued depreciation plus the land value.

> **Replacement cost** - cost of restoring a property to its previous condition or replacing it with something of like-kind and quality

> **Reproduction cost** - cost of replacing the improvement with one that is the exact replica, having the same quality of workmanship, design, and layout

Depreciation

Depreciation - loss in value from any cause

Accrued depreciation - difference between the cost to replace the property and the property's current appraised value

Straight-line (age-life) method is the most common method used to calculate accrued depreciation.

Actual age is the real age of the building. **Effective age** is the current condition and usefulness of the building. **Economic life (useful life)** is the length of time during which a piece of property may earn sufficient income to justify its continued existence.

Types of Depreciation

1. Physical Deterioration
2. Functional Obsolescence
3. Economic/Environmental Obsolescence

Physical deterioration and functional obsolescence can be curable or incurable.

> **Curable**   cost to cure is less than the value added to the property
>
> **Incurable**   cost to cure is greater than the value added to the property

Physical Deterioration

Physical Deterioration is the loss of value due to wear and tear, negligent care (sometimes called deferred maintenance), damage by dry rot or termites, or severe changes in temperature.

Functional Obsolescence

Functional Obsolescence is poor architectural design and style, lack of modern facilities, out-of-date equipment, changes in styles of construction, or changes in utility demand.

Economic or External Obsolescence

Economic or External Obsolescence occurs because of forces outside the property. It is usually incurable.

Income Approach

Income approach estimates the present worth of future benefits by capitalizing the income stream of a property. It is based on the principles of anticipation, substitution, and comparison. The income approach is used on income-producing properties.

Contract rent - rent actually paid by a tenant for use of the premises and may or may not be the same as economic rent

Economic rent - rent the property would command in an open market

Scheduled Gross Income - all of the income a property should produce

> **Vacancy / credit loss** - loss of revenue due to vacancies or uncollectible income. When expressed as a percentage it is a **vacancy rate**.
>
> **Effective Gross Income** - the difference between the scheduled gross income and the vacancy and credit loss

Operating Expenses - ordinary and necessary costs to the operation of an incoming producing property, does **not** include mortgage interest or IRS depreciation

Net Operating Income (NOI) - income available after paying operating expenses, but before paying debt

Capitalization of Income

Capitalization is the conversion of an income stream into an indication of value.

Capitalization (CAP) Rate - annual rate of return produced by an income producing property or the desired rate of return by an investor.

Formulas Used to Estimate the Value of an Income Property

- NOI divided by the Cap Rate equals the Value of the Property.
- NOI divided by Value of Property equals Cap Rate.

Income Multipliers

A **multiplier** is a number that, when multiplied by the income, gives an indicator of value. The value is based on income without expenses being deducted.

Gross Rent Multiplier (GRM) - figure which, when multiplied by the **monthly gross rental income**, will give an indication of the property's market value.

Value = GRM × Gross Monthly Rental Income

Gross Income Multiplier (GIM) - figure which, when multiplied by the **annual gross income from all sources**, will give an indication of the property's market value. The gross income could include parking, laundry, or fees for other services offered.

Value = GIM × Gross Annual Income from All Sources

CHAPTER 10 – REVIEW

Multiple-Choice Questions

1. The relationship between a thing desired and a potential purchaser is one definition of:
   a. economic function.
   b. economic necessity.
   c. effective public demand.
   d. value.

2. Which of the following is a correct statement about the approaches to valuations?
   a. The income approach is the preferred method to value real estate bought and sold on its ability to produce a financial return
   b. The sales comparison approach is the only approach that may be used with residential property
   c. In the cost approach, it is not necessary to consider the value of the land
   d. A study of reproduction costs is necessary to the income approach

3. Which of the following would be the most effective method in appraising single-family residences?
   a. The income approach
   b. The market data approach
   c. A competitive market analysis
   d. The cost approach

4. Economic or external obsolescence can result from:
   a. adverse changes in the economy.
   b. the construction of a freeway.
   c. paying more than the property was worth.
   d. the property has a negative cash flow.

5. The highest and best use of a property is use that gives the owner the greatest:
   a. gross return on money or amenities.
   b. value after a given period of time.
   c. net return on money or amenities.
   d. resale value.

6. The price a property would bring if freely offered on the open market, with both a willing buyer and a willing seller, is known as the:
   a. fair market value.
   b. listing offer.
   c. asking price.
   d. offer.

7. The value of real property is best measured by:
   a. demand, depreciation, scarcity, and utility.
   b. cost, demand, transferability, and utility.
   c. cost, feasibility, scarcity, and utility.
   d. demand, scarcity, transferability, and utility.

8. In the appraisal of real property, the term unearned increment refers to a(n):
    a. increase in value due to population increase.
    b. decrease in value due to social forces rather than personal effort.
    c. decrease of property taxes.
    d. depreciation.

9. Which of the following appraisal approaches is based on the principle of substitution?
    a. Replacement cost
    b. Reproduction cost
    c. Market comparison
    d. Capitalization

10. In determining the value on an unimproved parcel of land, the first thing to establish is the:
    a. listing price.
    b. purchase price.
    c. highest and best use.
    d. closest comparable properties.

11. In a well-planned residential community, what contributes most to the maintenance of value?
    a. Conformity to proper land-use objectives
    b. Deed restrictions
    c. Variances to permit the highest and best use of every parcel of land
    d. Prevention of major thoroughfare construction through the community

12. In appraising the value of a building using the replacement-cost approach, an appraiser would consider all of the following, except:
    a. the cost of improvements to the land.
    b. a separate estimate for the value of the land.
    c. allowances for depreciation.
    d. the appropriate capitalization rate.

13. Functional obsolescence would not include:
    a. eccentric design.
    b. items of surplus utility.
    c. lack of air conditioning.
    d. proximity to nuisances.

14. Economic rent is best defined as the rent:
    a. required to produce a suitable return for the owner.
    b. generated by the property in a theoretically perfectly informed market.
    c. agreed to by a lessor and lessee under the terms of a written lease.
    d. received for comparable space in the competitive open market.

15. To calculate a gross rent multiplier accurately, what does the appraiser need from comparable properties?
    a. Net income and selling price
    b. Original cost and the annual income
    c. Annual rent and the selling price
    d. Net income and the capitalization rate

16. The effective annual gross income of a property is the difference between the annual scheduled gross income and the _____.
    a. vacancy factor and rent collection losses
    b. allowable expenses and depreciation
    c. capitalization rate
    d. administrative expenses and capital improvements

17. What is the estimated period over which a building may be profitably used known as?
    a. Earning period
    b. Economic life
    c. Investment period
    d. Productive life

18. Which of these would be used by an appraiser who has chosen the income approach to establish the value of an apartment building?
    a. Excess rent
    b. Percentage rent
    c. Economic rent
    d. Contract rent

19. A 12-year-old building in excellent condition is given an age of 6 years by an appraiser. This would be known as its:
    a. actual age.
    b. economic life.
    c. effective age.
    d. physical life.

20. The gross rent multiplier is defined as:
    a. sales value divided by gross rent.
    b. gross rent divided by sales value.
    c. assessed value divided by gross rent.
    d. gross rent divided by market value.

Answer Key

1. (d) Value or worth is the present and future anticipated enjoyment or profit from the ownership of property. It is the relationship between the thing desired and the purchaser.

2. (a) The value of income producing property is based on the property's ability to generate a return on the investment.

3. (b) The market data or sales comparison approach is given the most weight and used primarily for appraising single-family residences.

4. (b) Economic obsolescence results from forces outside of the property that negatively affect value.

5. (c) The highest and best use of a property generates the greatest net return on the investment.

6. (a) The price a property would bring if freely offered on the open market, with both a willing buyer and a willing seller, is known as fair market value—or market value.

7. (d) There are four elements of value, all of which must be present for a property to have market value. They are demand, utility, scarcity, and transferability.

8. (a) Unearned increment refers to the increase in the value of a property due to a population influx. This increases the amount of goods and services available and leads to additional infrastructure and overall growth.

9. (c) The market comparison approach uses the principle of substitution to compare similar properties.

10. (c) At the end of an appraisal, an appraiser must be prepared to answer the following two questions: 1. What is the highest and best use of the property? 2. What is this use worth?

11. (a) When land uses are compatible and homes are similar in design and size, the maximum value is realized. Conformity (similarity) upholds neighborhood values. Where there are mixed homes, unstable real estate values may occur.

12. (d) The capitalization rate represents the annual return on an investment.

13. (d) Poor architectural design and style can contribute to functional obsolescence, as can lack of modern facilities, out-of-date equipment, changes in styles of construction, or changes in utility demand. For instance, a four-bedroom house with only one bathroom might be considered functionally obsolete because most homes today have at least two bathrooms with many having one bath for each bedroom. It may or may not be curable.

14. (d) Economic rent, or the amount the rental could bring in an open market.

15. (c) The GRM compares properties to see if they are priced right or are above or below market value. If you know that most rental properties are selling for around eight times the gross annual multiplier (eight times gross), simply divide the listed price by the gross income to arrive at the multiplier.

16. (a) The effective gross income is the total annual income from the property minus any vacancy or rental losses.

17. (b) Economic life is the estimated period over which a building may be profitably used.

18. (c) An appraiser valuating a property looks at the economic rent, rather than the contract rent, in order to discover the fair income of the property.

19. (c) Effective age is not determined by the actual age of a building but by its condition and usefulness.

20. (a) Divide the list price by the gross annual income.

Chapter 11
Land Use, Subdivisions, & Housing

Communities try to ensure quality places to work and live by using the tools at hand: subdivision regulations, city master plans, zoning laws, and building codes.

Four Types of Government Controls
Mnemonic = PETE

Police power

Escheat

Taxation

Eminent Domain

Eminent domain - power of the government to take private property for the public use after paying **just compensation** to the owner

Police power - power of the state to enact laws (within constitutional limits) to promote the order, safety, health, morals, and general welfare of our society

PLANNING & DEVELOPMENT

Comprehensive plan - basis of and sets the direction for a community's future development.

Zoning

The regulation of structures and uses of property within selected districts is known as **zoning**. Frequently, buffer zones are used between divergent land uses. A **buffer zone** is an area or strip of land, which separates one zoning use from another.

Spot zoning allows a needed use in a neighborhood that does not conform to the existing zoning.

A municipality may allow a **variance**, or an exception to existing zoning regulations, for special reasons. A variance is not a non-conforming use.

Zoning changes can create a **non-conforming use** in non-compliance with existing zoning rules. If existing, may continue to operate under a **grandfather clause**.

Examples of Zoning: Agricultural, Commercial, 4 Units/High Density Dwellings, Offices (Low/Mid/High Rise), Manufacturing (Industrial), Public Use, Single Family Residential, Planned Unit Developments, Duplexes, Multi-Residential/Apartments

Subdivision

State and local governments regulate the development of subdivisions.

A **subdivision** is the division of land into lots for the purpose of sale, lease, or finance.

A **subdivider** buys undeveloped land and divides it into smaller lots for sale.

A **developer** improves land, constructs buildings on land, and sells them.

Types of Subdivisions

Typical subdivisions include standard subdivisions and common interest developments.

A **standard subdivision** is a land division with no common or mutual rights of either ownership or use among the owners of the parcels created by the division. This type of subdivision is a typical tract of single-family homes on individual lots.

A **common interest development (CID)** combines the individual ownership of private dwellings with the shared ownership of common facilities of the entire project. The CID is governed by a community association, sometimes called a **homeowners' association (HOA)**.

A **condominium** consists of a separate fee interest in a particular specific space (the unit), plus an undivided interest in all common or public areas of the development. All owners are allowed to use any of the facilities in the common area. Each unit owner has a deed, separate financing, and pays the property taxes for their unit.

A **planned development** is a planning and zoning term describing land not subject to conventional zoning requirements.

Deed restrictions or CC&Rs (covenants, conditions, and restrictions) are private land use controls usually put in place by the developer of a subdivision.

Laches is an unreasonable delay by a party making a claim or bringing an action, so that the rights of said parties are waived. There is no statute of limitations. The concept of laches can be applied to delayed enforcement of deed restrictions.

The **Environmental Impact Statement (EIS)** is a study of the potential effects a proposed project will have on such things as pollution, population density, energy consumption, community and employment trends, and the environment.

HOUSING & CONSTRUCTION

The housing and construction industries are regulated by local building codes and state laws. Construction and development is monitored by issuing **building permits** and then inspecting the buildings during construction to make sure the building codes are met.

As a requirement for FHA and VA financing, the house involved must meet **Minimum Property Requirements (MPRs).**

Unless a real estate licensee works for a builder/developer or specializes in new home sales, it is not usually necessary to know the details of home construction, installation methods, or the price and quality of building materials. However, a licensee should be familiar with architectural styles, types of roofs, styles of windows, parts of a building, typical exterior materials, and different types of heating/cooling systems (HVAC).

Types of Lots

The type of lot helps determine the type of improvement that will be built.

Corner lot is found at the intersection of two streets. It may be desirable because of its accessibility, but may also be noisy and expensive to maintain because of the increased frontage.

Cul-de-sac is sometimes known as dead-end street. It is a street with only one way in or out. This may be desirable because of the privacy and quietness, but the lot may be undesirable if oddly pie-shaped on the turn-around section of the street.

Flag lot looks like a flag on a pole. The pole represents the access to the site, which is usually located to the rear of another lot fronting a main street.

Interior lot is surrounded by other lots, with frontage on the street. It is the most common type lot and may be desirable or not, depending on other factors.

Key lot is surrounded by the backyards of other lots. It is the least desirable because of the lack of privacy.

T-intersection lot is fronted head-on by a street. The noise and glare from headlights may detract from this type of lot.

Building Standards

Building Codes are rules and regulations that regulate the construction and occupancy of buildings for health and safety reasons.

Setbacks are the distance a building must be set back from the street, property line, or curb. They are usually determined by local building code.

A **side-yard setback** is the distance a building must be set back for the lot line at the side of the property.

Some homes are built on lots with no side-yard setback, called a **zero lot-line** property. The home is built directly on the lot's boundary line.

Energy Efficiency

A licensee should be able to answer questions about current insulation standards for roofs, walls, and window systems that prevent excess sun infiltration for homes in the area.

Energy Efficiency Terms

- **Insulation:** Material inserted into walls and ceilings to help keep the heat inside the home in the winter and outside the home in the summer.

  Some older homes may have urea-formaldehyde foam insulation installed. **Urea-formaldehyde** is a chemical organic compound found in building materials, which may be a carcinogen. It is no longer used in building materials.

- **R-value:** The R-value is a rating that measures how well insulation resists heat loss. When the R-value is higher, the insulation is better. New homes have minimum insulation requirements and the R-value rating of the insulation used in the homes must be disclosed.

- **Energy Efficient Ratio (EER):** A measurement of the efficiency of energy. It is used to determine the effectiveness of appliances.

Parts of a Building
Common Building Terms

1. **Anchor Bolt**
Attaches mudsill to foundation; embedded in concrete foundation

2. **Bracing**
Diagonal board nailed across wall framing to prevent sway

3. **Building Paper**
Waterproof paper used between sheathing and roof covering

4. **Closed Sheathing**
Foundation for exterior siding; boards nailed to studding

5. **Crawlspace**
A crawlspace is the area or space between the ground and floor joists used to access plumbing and electrical connections beneath the house. For FHA loans, the minimum crawlspace is 18 inches.

6. **Cripple**
Studs above a window or door header or below a windowsill

7. **Eaves**
Part of roof that hangs over the exterior walls

8. **Fire Stop**
Boards nailed between studs to block the spread of fire in the walls

9. **Flashing**
Sheet metal or other material that keeps water from seeping into a building

10. **Footing**
A footing is an extended part of foundation at the base or bottom of a foundation wall, pier, or column.

11. **Foundation**
Base of house; usually concrete

12. **Header**
The horizontal, load-bearing board over a doorway or window opening

13. **Joists**
Parallel boards supporting floors or ceilings (The boards supporting them are girders, beams, or bearing walls.)

14. **Mud Sill**
The lowest part of the frame of a house. It is fastened with bolts to the foundation and supports the upright studs of the frame.

15. **Open Sheathing**
Boards nailed to rafters to form foundation for roof

16. **Rafters**
Slanted boards of a roof that are designed to support the roof boards and shingles. To strengthen the load-bearing factor of a roof, the rafters should be placed closer together.

17. **Ridge Board**
Highest structural part of a frame building

18. **Sill**
Horizontal board along the bottom of a window or door

19. **Sole Plate**
A board, usually 2" x 4", on which wall and partition studs rest.

20. **Studs**
Vertical, supporting 2"x 4" boards in the walls spaced 16" on center

Roof Types

Roof types are determined by the direction, steepness, and number of roof planes. The **pitch** of a roof is its incline or rise.

A **flat roof** has a very low pitch.

A **gable roof** has a pitched roof with two sloping sides.

A **shed roof** is half of a gable roof.

A **gambrel roof**, typically seen in Dutch colonial architecture, is a curbed roof, with a steep lower slope with a flatter one above.

A **hip roof** is a pitched roof with sloping sides and ends (all four sides).

A **mansard roof** is a roof with two slopes to all four sides and usually envelopes the top floor of the building.

Windows

Windows allow light into a house, improve airflow, and keep weather out. **Windowpanes** are held in place by window frames and sashes, which are made of wood, metal, vinyl, or fiberglass.

Most windowpanes are conventional glass but some may be laminated glass, tempered glass, or even wired-glass. Windows also come in single-glazed, dual-glazed, or even triple-glazed varieties.

Types of Windows

A single house may use a variety of window types. Windows are described by their glazing patterns, shape, placement in the house, and the way they open.

Fixed windows do not open or move at all. **Skylights** are a type of fixed window. Skylights are estimated to let five times more light into a house than another window of the same size. Skylights also help a space look much larger than it is and add value to the house.

Traverse windows slide from side to side. **Sliding glass doors** are simply large, traverse windows.

Single-hung windows - bottom portion slides up.

Double-hung windows - both top and bottom parts move up and down.

Casement windows - have hinges on the sides and open with cranks.

Awning window - hinged at the top and opens out.

Hopper window - hinged at the bottom and opens into the room.

Jalousie windows - narrow glass slats like Venetian blinds that are opened and closed with a crank. They do not slide or use a hinge.

Wall Material (Cladding)

Cladding includes the external protective skin of the exterior surfaces of a home (surface coatings, siding, doors, windows, trim, shutters, entryways, and flashings). The cladding for exterior walls includes surface coatings, such as paint and varnish, and all types of siding, stucco, brick, stone, adobe, concrete, metal panels, and plate glass with steel.

Siding refers to overlapping horizontal boards made from wood, vinyl, or aluminum that are applied to the house. Sometimes a house has **board and batten**, which is an application of vertical boards with joints that are finished by thin vertical strips.

House Styles

Traditional house styles used in building are interesting for their variety and important for a real estate agent to know. Common house styles include Bungalow, Cape Cod, Colonial, Mediterranean, Pueblo, Ranch, Tudor, and Victorian.

CHAPTER 11 – REVIEW

Multiple-Choice Questions

1. Which of the following rights can be vested in an individual?
   a. Police power
   b. Escheat
   c. Riparian
   d. Eminent domain

2. A grandfather clause:
   a. is a change in zoning.
   b. is an example of down zoning.
   c. permits continuation of a nonconforming use.
   d. is an inheritance right to property.

3. A builder is allowed to make a change in construction that does not conform to the local building code. This is an example of:
   a. rezoning.
   b. a variance.
   c. a conditional-use permit.
   d. a restriction.

4. A small area zoned differently from the surrounding area is called:
   a. a variance.
   b. spot zoning.
   c. non-conforming use.
   d. off-zoning.

5. The generic term for a strip of land separating two types of land use is:
   a. buffer zone.
   b. variance.
   c. non-conforming use.
   d. divider zone.

6. City ordinances dictating how structures and other types of improvement can be built, specifying the quality of materials, the designs, and the construction standards to be used, are:
   a. Subdivision restrictions.
   b. Community Reinvestment Rules.
   c. Appraisal Board Rules.
   d. Building Codes.

7. The R-value is a rating that measures:
   a. how well insulation resists heat loss.
   b. the efficiency of energy, used to determine the effectiveness of appliances.
   c. the amount of heat needed to raise one pound of water one degree Fahrenheit.
   d. insulation.

8. The delay in asserting one's rights is called:
    a.   laches.
    b.   negligence.
    c.   fee limitation.
    d.   a legal impediment.

9. Which is not part of a building's foundation?
    a.   Anchor bolts
    b.   Footing
    c.   Mudsill
    d.   Ridge board

10. The words, gambrel, hip, gable, and flat refer to types of:
    a.   houses.
    b.   conduit.
    c.   insulation.
    d.   roofs.

Answer Key

1. (c) The four types of government controls are police power, escheat, taxation, and eminent domain. Individual property owners can own riparian rights.

2. (c) When an area is rezoned to another use, existing properties may retain the previous zoning under a grandfather clause.

3. (b) A city or county may allow a variance, or an exception to existing zoning regulations for special reasons.

4. (b) Spot zoning is the rezoning of a small area incompatible to the surrounding use. It normally only benefits the property owners.

5. (a) The correct term for this piece of land is a buffer zone.

6. (d) Building codes will dictate how properties are built and developed.

7. (a) The R-value is a rating that measures how well insulation resists heat loss.

8. (a) Laches is an unreasonable delay by a party making a claim or bringing an action, so that the right of said parties is waived. There is no statute of limitations.

9. (d) The ridge board is the highest structural part of a frame building.

10. (d) A gable roof has a pitched roof with two sloping sides. A gambrel roof, typically seen in Dutch colonial architecture, is a curbed roof, with a steep lower slope with a flatter one above. A hip roof is a pitched roof with sloping sides and ends (all four sides).

Chapter 12
Real Estate Brokerage

The term **brokerage** generally means an activity involving the sale of something through a go-between who negotiates the transaction for payment. In the case of a real estate brokerage, the product is real property, with the broker as negotiator and agent of the principal, expecting a commission at the end of the negotiation. The **broker** is a **special agent** of the principal (seller or buyer) and the salesperson is a **general agent** of his or her broker.

BUSINESS OWNERSHIP

A real estate broker may open a real estate brokerage in his or her name, or a fictitious business name. The broker may have multiple locations and take ownership in a variety of ways, such as sole proprietorship, partnership, corporation, or limited liability company (LLC).

Sole proprietorship - business owned and operated by one person. The owner is personally and fully liable for all business debts. The broker reports all debts and reports any income or loss directly on his or her personal income tax return.

Partnership - business in which two or more persons join their money and skills in conducting the business. Just like a sole proprietorship, the broker-owners of a partnership are jointly and severally liable for all business debts. **Joint and several liability** is a legal term used in reference to a debt, in which each debtor is responsible for the entire amount of the debt. Partnerships do not file tax returns. All partnership income, expenses, gains, and losses pass through to the individual partners to be reported on their personal income tax returns.

Corporation - legal entity with business rights similar to an individual. A corporation exists indefinitely; it has centralized management in a board of directors; its shareholder liability is limited to the amount of their individual investment; and its corporate stocks are freely transferred. A corporation files an income tax return in its own name.

Limited liability company (LLC) - alternative business entity that has characteristics of both corporations and limited partnerships. The LLC offers its owners the advantage of limited personal liability (like a corporation) and a choice of how the business will be taxed. Partners can choose for the LLC to be taxed as a separate entity (like a corporation) or as a partnership-like entity in which profits are passed through to partners and taxed on their personal income tax returns.

Measuring Profitability of the Brokerage Firm

The owner of the brokerage firm needs to know how much money is available to operate the business and how much each sales associate must produce to cover office expenses. Two quick ways the broker can determine profitability are the company dollar and the desk cost.

The **company dollar** is the amount a broker has left after all commissions have been paid. The **desk cost** shows how much each sales associate must earn to cover expenses. It is calculated by dividing the total operating expenses of the firm by the number of licensed sales associates. A profit margin for the broker is not included as an operating expense.

EMPLOYMENT RELATIONSHIPS

An **employee** is defined as someone who is under the control and direction of an employer. An **independent contractor** is a person hired to work for another person, but is not an employee of that person.

Tests Used to Determine Independent Contractor Status

- Must be a **written contract** between the sponsoring broker and the salesperson.

- Valid real estate license

- Salesperson must be compensated on the basis of the number of sales closed and commissions earned—not on the basis of the number of hours worked.

A salesperson can be paid only by his or her sponsoring broker. A salesperson cannot receive compensation or referral fees directly from a lender, developer, buyer, or seller.

The listings and any buyer representation agreements belong to the original broker.

REAL ESTATE SIGNS & PROSPECTING

Displaying real estate signs has some protection under the United States statutes as a form of free speech. A city, county, or private entity, such as a homeowners' association, may regulate the size of signs and how they are displayed. Private real estate signs may be banned completely from public property. However, a homeowners' association or deed restrictions cannot prohibit private owners from displaying real estate signs on their own property.

Sign Regulations

- A city, county, or state may ban all signs on publicly owned property.

- A city, county, or state cannot completely ban signs on privately owned property.

- A city, county, or state may impose reasonable restrictions on the time, place, and manner of displaying signs regardless of whether it is on privately or publicly owned property.

Prospecting is the process of identifying potential customers. The majority of sales associates prospect by cold calling or sending text through mailings, faxes, or e-mails. **Cold calling** involves making unsolicited calls to people you do not know in order to get new business.

Anytime real estate solicitation involves the use of the telephone, cell phone, fax, or e-mail, the sales associate must comply with applicable federal "do not call" and "CAN-SPAM" laws. You may still call, fax, and e-mail potential clients but you must follow certain procedures.

FAIR HOUSING LAWS

Real estate licensees must be aware of federal and state fair housing laws and issues, and apply this knowledge daily. By learning the fair housing laws, including advertising guidelines, your job will be made easier.

Federal Laws

1866 Civil Rights Act

This federal law prohibits discrimination based on race in all property transactions. However, it was ignored until 1968.

Fair Housing Act

Title VIII of the Civil Rights Act of 1968, as amended in 1974 and 1988, constitutes the Fair Housing Act. Under these laws, real estate offices are required to display Fair Housing posters. Complaints are filed with HUD.

The **Fair Housing Act** prohibits discrimination in the sale, rental, and financing of dwellings, and in other housing-related transactions, based on federally mandated protected classes.

Protected Classes Under the Federal Fair Housing Act

- Race
- Color
- National origin
- Religion
- Sex
- Familial status
- Handicap

Age is not protected under the Fair Housing Act.

Actions Prohibited by the Fair Housing Act

- Refusing to rent or sell housing
- Altering terms and conditions
- Advertising a discriminatory housing preference or limitation
- Providing false information about the availability of housing
- **Steering** - guiding persons to or away from a specific neighborhood
- **Blockbusting** - persuading an owner to sell or rent housing by saying that people of a particular race, religion, etc., are moving into the neighborhood

Enforcement of the Fair Housing Act

HUD has the authority of enforcement on the federal level. If one is accused of discrimination, failure to display the Fair Housing Poster is prima facie evidence of guilt.

1968 U.S. Supreme Court Case of Jones v. Mayer

Jones v. Mayer prohibits discrimination based on race by upholding the 1866 Civil Rights Act and the 13th Amendment to the U.S. Constitution prohibiting slavery.

Americans with Disabilities Act (ADA)

The **Americans with Disabilities Act (ADA)** protects anyone with a handicap and includes mental illness, AIDS, blindness, hearing impairment, mental retardation, and mobility impairment.

A **handicap** is defined as any physical or mental impairment which substantially limits one or more major life activities, having a record of such an impairment, or being regarded as having such an impairment.

ADA affects employers and their employment policies. They must make reasonable accommodations to allow individuals with a disability to perform their employment responsibilities.

Title III of ADA affects access to business and public accommodations.

Antitrust Laws

Price/Commission Fixing

Price fixing is an agreement between business competitors to sell the same product or service at the same price. Real estate brokers may not engage in price fixing. This means that two or more competing real estate firms may not agree on the commission rates that each will charge. However, a broker may set the office policy and commission rates that are to be followed by his or her sale associates.

Agreements as to Other Listing Terms

Competitors should not create nor suggest that any of the following agreements regarding employment contracts (listing and buyer representation agreements) are in place.

- The length of the listing or buyer's representation agreement
- The type of listing accepted
- The marketing services to be provided by the listing broker
- Taking listings in defined (by agreement) geographic areas

Boycotts

A **boycott** is the act of abstaining from using, buying, or dealing with an organization as an expression of protest or as a means of coercion. In real estate, a **group boycott** is an agreement among competitors not to do business with a particular business or another competitor. The object of this type of agreement would be to change the competitor's behavior or drive a competitor out of business.

Monopolies

A **monopoly** is a market condition with only one provider of goods or services, which could create higher prices. The **Sherman Antitrust Act** was passed in 1890 to limit monopolies. The Act was intended to prevent the artificial raising of prices by restriction of trade or supply due to a monopoly of the market.

CHAPTER 12 – REVIEW

Multiple-Choice Questions

1. Which type of business ownership is always taxed as a separate entity and files its own income tax return?
   a. Sole proprietorship
   b. Partnership
   c. Corporation
   d. Limited liability company

2. A broker uses a profitability measurement called _____ to determine how much each sales associate must earn to cover the brokerage expenses.
   a. joint and several responsibility
   b. company dollar
   c. desk cost
   d. intermediation

3. Of the following, which is a test used to determine independent contractor status of a sales associate?
   a. There must be a written contract between the sponsoring broker and the sales associate.
   b. Sales associate must have valid real estate license.
   c. Sales associate must be compensated on the basis of the number of sales closed and commissions earned—not on the basis of the number of hours worked.
   d. All of the above.

4. Which statement regarding real estate signs is incorrect?
   a. A homeowners' association can prohibit private owners from displaying real estate signs on their own property.
   b. A city, county or state may ban all signs on publicly owned property.
   c. A city, county, or state cannot completely ban signs on privately owned property.
   d. A city, county, or state may impose reasonable restrictions on the time, place, and manner of displaying signs regardless of whether it is on privately or publicly owned property.

5.   Real estate ads should not have words stating or implying a preference with regard to on race, color, national origin, religion, sex, familial status, or handicap. If used in an advertisement, which of the following phrases would be incorrect?
     a.   Gated community
     b.   Parks nearby
     c.   Catholic church nearby
     d.   Great shopping

6.   Gary just took a listing on a three-bedroom fixer-upper home located in an area with very good schools. It is a mixed neighborhood, although it is primarily Hispanic. Gary wrote several ads to market the home. Which ad does not follow acceptable advertising guidelines?
     a.   This is the best home in the neighborhood and in a good school district.
     b.   Nice fixer, located by parks and good schools with three-bedrooms.
     c.   Clean, bright, and move-in ready for the right family.
     d.   Beautiful home near parks, looking for Hispanic family.

7.   The illegal practice of telling people that property values in a neighborhood will decline because of a specific event, such as the purchase of homes by minorities, is called:
     a.   blockbusting.
     b.   steering.
     c.   redlining.
     d.   panicking.

8.   The Fair Housing Act does not prohibit discrimination in the sale, rental, and financing of dwellings based on:
     a.   age.
     b.   color.
     c.   familial status.
     d.   religion.

9.   Which of the following statements would not be a violation of anti-trust laws?
     a.   Our local realty association has a minimum commission policy.
     b.   This is the standard commission rate in our community.
     c.   My office policy is not to accept listings for less than 90 days.
     d.   MLS will not accept a listing that pays less than 6% commission.

10. The act of abstaining from using, buying, or dealing with an organization as an expression of protest or as a means of coercion is:
     a.   a monopoly.
     b.   boycott.
     c.   price fixing.
     d.   steering.

Answer Key

1. (c) In a sole proprietorship and partnership, all income, expenses, gains, and losses are reported on the owners personal income tax returns. The LLC may choose how the business will be taxed—as a separate entity (like a corporation) or as a partnership-like entity in which profits are passed through to partners and taxed on their personal income tax returns. Corporations are taxed as a separate entity.

2. (c) The company dollar is the amount a broker has left after all commissions have been paid. The desk cost shows how much each sales associate must earn to cover expenses.

3. (d) Tests used to determine independent contractor status—must be a written contract between the sponsoring broker and the salesperson, valid real estate license, salesperson must be compensated on the basis of the number of sales closed and commissions earned—not on the basis of the number of hours worked.

4. (a) A city, county, or state may ban all signs on publicly owned property. A city, county, or state cannot completely ban signs on privately owned property. A city, county, or state may impose reasonable restrictions on the time, place, and manner of displaying signs regardless of whether it is on privately or publicly owned property.

5. (c) Real estate advertisements should not have words that state or imply a preference or limitation with regard to race, color, religion, handicap, sex, or familial status.

6. (d) Real estate ads should not include words stating or implying a preference or limitation with regard to race, color, religion, handicap, sex, or familial status.

7. (a) Blockbusting or panic peddling is persuading an owner to sell or rent housing by saying that people of a particular race, religion, etc., are moving into the neighborhood.

8. (a) The Fair Housing Act prohibits discrimination in the sale, rental, and financing of dwellings, and in other housing-related transactions, based on race, color, national origin, religion, sex, familial status, and handicap. Age is not protected under the Fair Housing Act.

9. (c) Brokers are allowed to set whatever policies they desire within their own office.

10. (b) A boycott is the act of abstaining from using, buying, or dealing with an organization as an expression of protest or as a means of coercion.

Chapter 13
Real Estate Specialization

BUSINESS OPPORTUNITY BROKERAGE

REALTORS® often get involved with the sale of a business because, if real property is one of the assets of the business, a real estate license is required to execute the sale.

A **business opportunity** is any type of business for lease or sale. It also includes **goodwill**, which is the expectation of the continued patronage of an existing business.

The sale of a business is considered the sale of personal property and the rules about the transfer of chattels are applied.

The sale of a business deals with these elements: (1) real property, (2) personal property, (3) assumption of liabilities, and (4) intangible assets. Each of the elements in the sale has value and must be considered when listing a business opportunity.

Real Property. Some interest in real property owned by the business is transferred. The business may own the building where the business is located or have an assignable lease that is included in the sale.

Personal Property. Personal property of business includes inventory, equipment, stock, and fixtures.

Assumption of Liabilities. As part of the sale, a buyer may assume short-term (current) liabilities or long-term liabilities. A **short-term liability** is a debt coming within a year or less, such as accounts payable. A **long-term liability** is a debt coming due in more than one year, such as a mortgage or loan for a vehicle.

Intangible Assets. Intangible assets that may be included in the sale are goodwill, franchises, licenses, patents, and copyrights. **Goodwill** is the reputation of the business and the expectation of the continued patronage of an existing business.

Regulating the Sale of a Business Opportunity

Certain legal requirements must be met in the sale of a business. Some laws, like the Uniform Commercial Code, are the same in all states. Laws concerning sales and use taxes and the transfer of a liquor license, vary from state to state.

Uniform Commercial Code

Whenever money has been borrowed for the sale of a business opportunity, it follows that someone has a security interest in the personal property belonging to the business. These transactions are regulated by the **Uniform Commercial Code (UCC)** Divisions 6 and 9.

Bulk Sales

Bulk sales, or the sale of a substantial part of the inventory of a business, are regulated by Division 6 of the UCC. The purpose of the Bulk Transfer Act is to protect the creditors of a person who sells a business. When a business is sold and most or all of the inventory, supplies, and other materials are transferred with the sale, public notice must be given. Any bulk sale that takes place without complying with the requirements of the **bulk transfer law** is considered valid between the buyer and seller but fraudulent and void against creditors. Therefore, the buyer is liable to creditors who hold valid claims based on transactions or events occurring before the bulk transfer sale.

Security Transactions in Personal Property and Fixtures

Division 9 of the UCC sets out the requirements for regulating security transactions in personal property and fixtures. The documents used are the promissory note, the security agreement, and the financing statement.

Sales and Use Tax

Sales and use tax laws protect a buyer from liability for unpaid sales tax owed by the seller. Sales and use tax are mutually exclusive, which means that a person will either pay sales tax or use tax, but not both. **Sales tax** is collected as a percentage of the retail sale of a product, by a retailer. **Use tax** is a tax imposed on the buyer who purchases goods from an out-of-state supplier and brings those good into another state within six months of the purchase date.

Liquor License

Whenever transfer of a liquor license is involved in a business opportunity sale, a buyer must not assume an automatic transfer of the liquor license. A buyer must apply for the license and be approved by the state agency that regulates these licenses.

INVESTING IN REAL ESTATE

Why invest in Real Estate? Historically, real property has shown consistent growth in value and remains the best **hedge against inflation**. Compared to other investments, real estate is not liquid. **Liquidity** refers to the ease in which an asset can be converted into cash.

The four main benefits of investment real estate are: (1) appreciation, (2) equity buildup, (3) income, and (4) tax benefits.

1. **Appreciation** is an increase in property value with the passage of time. **Leverage** is the use of borrowed capital to buy real estate. An **unearned increment** is the increase in value due to market forces.

2. **Equity buildup** is the gradual increase of the borrower's equity in a property caused by amortization of loan principal.

3. **Income (cash flow)**
    Most investors look for a return on their investment.
    RETURN **ON** the investment (Interest)
    RETURN **OF** the investment (Recapture)

4. **Tax benefits**
    Depreciation is a deductible non-cash expense based on the IRS determined life of the property.

    A **capital gain** is the taxable profit (usually at a tax-favored rate) that is made from the sale of a capital asset. The **cost basis** is usually the original purchase price of the property. When capital improvements are added to the original cost basis, the **adjusted cost basis** is the result.

    The **taxable gain** generally is the difference between the purchase price plus capital improvements and the price when sold.

    An **installment sale** is one in which payments are made by the buyer to the seller, over a period of more than one year.

    The **1031 Deferred Exchange**, sometimes called a tax-free exchange, is a method of deferring federal income tax liability.

TIMESHARE PROPERTIES

A **timeshare** is a real estate development in which a buyer can purchase the exclusive right to occupy a unit for a specified time period each year. The time is usually in one-week intervals and can be a fixed week or a floating week. In addition to the one-time purchase price, timeshare owners pay an annual fee for property management and maintenance. Timeshares are usually resort-type subdivisions created with the intention of selling them to people who want a retirement home or second, vacation home.

PROPERTY MANAGEMENT

The management of a property on behalf of the owner is called **property management**. The main goal of property management is to protect the owner's investment and maximize the owner's return on that investment.

Property managers can be **employees** of the owner, or **agents** for several owners.

A **real estate license** is required to manage property for an owner, unless the manager is an employee of the owner.

The **building manager**, employed by a property manager or the owner, usually manages a single building or office complex.

Resident managers are employed to manage an apartment building on either a part-time or a full-time basis.

Property Management Agreement

The **management agreement** shows the terms of the agreement between the owner and the property manager and creates a general agency relationship.

Management fees are negotiated and can be either a flat amount per month, a percentage of the gross rents collected, or a combination of the two.

Property Management Activities

Real estate licensing	Leasing agreements
Agency	Fair housing
Employment	Property protection
Insurance	Construction and repairs
Marketing	Business administration
Tenant/landlord relationships	Maintenance programs

CHAPTER 13 – REVIEW

Multiple-Choice Questions

1. Timeshare properties are primarily designed for buyers looking for:
   a. income-producing real property.
   b. vacation property.
   c. a primary residence.
   d. agricultural property.

2. The expectation of the continued patronage of an existing business is:
   a. goodwill.
   b. business opportunity.
   c. leverage.
   d. unearned increment.

3. Which of these would provide an investor with the best hedge against inflation?
   a. United States government bonds
   b. A savings account in a bank
   c. Ownership of real property
   d. A note secured by a first deed of trust

4. When investors are considering a real estate investment, they take into account:
   a. the potential for appreciation.
   b. equity build-up.
   c. the return on the investment.
   d. all of the above.

5. Value that increases with the passage of time is called:
   a. cash flow.
   b. leverage.
   c. depreciation.
   d. appreciation.

6. Which is the best example of leverage?
   a. Investing primarily personal funds
   b. Investing personal and borrowed funds equally
   c. Investing primarily borrowed funds
   d. Investing in properties with diminishing values

7. The taxable profit that is made from the sale of a capital asset is called:
   a. cost basis.
   b. depreciation.
   c. return of investment.
   d. capital gain.

8. The original purchase price of a property is called the:
   a. adjusted cost basis.
   b. capital gain.
   c. cost basis.
   d. taxable gain.

9. Real estate investors can defer federal income tax liability through:
   a. installment sales.
   b. tax-deferred exchanges.
   c. both (a) and (b).
   d. neither (a) nor (b).

10. The main goal of a property manager is to:
    a. protect the owner's investment.
    b. get the highest vacancy rate in the area.
    c. obtain 100% occupancy due to below market rents.
    d. minimize the owner's return on that investment.

Answer Key

1. (b) Timeshares are frequently purchased as a vacation investment because the cost of owning a good timeshare is less than renting comparable hotel accommodations year after year.

2. (a) Goodwill is the expectation of the continued patronage of an existing business.

3. (c) Historically, real property has shown a consistent growth in value and remains the best hedge against inflation. By owning assets that rise in value with inflation, e.g., real estate, an investor can beat inflation.

4. (d) Real estate investors look for appreciation, equity build-up, income, and tax benefits.

5. (d) Appreciation is an increase in property value with the passage of time.

6. (c) This is known as leverage—the use of borrowed capital to buy real estate. It is a process permitting the buyer to use little of one's own money and large amounts of someone else's money.

7. (d) A capital gain is the taxable profit (usually at a tax-favored rate) that is made from the sale of a capital asset.

8. (c) The cost basis is usually the original purchase price of the property. When capital improvements are added to the original cost basis, the adjusted cost basis is the result.

9. (c) Some tax advantages from real estate investment are installment sales and tax-deferred exchanges.

10. (a) The main goal of a property manager is to protect the owner's investment and maximize the owner's return on that investment.

Math: Bonus Section

INTRODUCTION

Math questions are distributed within the following areas

- Commission Problems
- Interest and Loan Problems
- Capitalization Problems
- Investment Problems
- Cost and Selling Price Problems
- Square Footage and Area Calculations

BASIC MATH PRINCIPLES

This section will explain the basic mathematical procedures you will need to be successful in your new real estate career.

Measurements

1 foot	12 inches
1 square foot	A unit of area equal to 1 foot by 1 foot square (144 square inches)
1 board foot	144 cubic inches (1 foot x 1 foot x 1 inch)
Square footage	Number of square feet of livable space in a home
Perimeter	Distance measured around the outside of a geometric shape
1 yard	36 inches or 3 feet
1 square yard	9 square feet
1 mile	5,280 feet or 320 rods
1 acre	43,560 square feet

Equivalent Amounts		
Percentage	**Decimal**	**Fraction**
4 1/2%	0.045	45/1000
6 2/3%	0.0667	1/15
10%	0.10	1/10
12 1/2%	0.125	1/8
16 2/3%	0.1667	1/6
25%	0.25	1/4
33 1/3%	0.33	1/3
50%	0.50	1/2
66 2/3%	0.667	2/3
75%	0.75	3/4
100%	1.00	1/1

Basic Math Circle

The math circle shows the relationship of the whole, part, and percentage rate.

Basic Real Estate Formulas

There are usually only three variables in any real estate problem—two things that are known and one that is unknown. From the information given in the problem, you must decide whether to multiply or divide the two numbers that you know in order to find the unknown third number. To use the basic math circle to solve real estate problems, rename the sections. Part is renamed Made, Whole is renamed Paid, and Rate is renamed Rate or Percentage. Whenever you have a math problem, one of these formulas probably can be used.

Three Variations of the "Made/Paid" Formula.

Made = Paid × Rate ($I = P \times R$)

Paid = Made ÷ Rate ($P = I \div R$)

Rate = Made ÷ Paid ($R = I \div P$)

Solving Real Estate Problems			
	MADE	**PAID**	**RATE**
	I	P	R
Commissions	Commission Income	Sales Price	Commission Rate
Loans	Interest	Principal	Interest Rate
Appraisal	Net operating Income	Property value	Cap Rate
Investment	Earned Income	Amount Paid	Rate of Return
Selling Price	Increase	Purchase Price	Rate of Profit
Seller's Net	Net Income	Sales Price	Commission Rate

Commission Problems

Commission problems involve these three variables:

Made **(I)** = Commission **I**ncome

Paid **(P)** = Selling **P**rice of the property

Rate **(R)** = Commission **R**ate

Practice Problem #1

Sara, a real estate salesperson, found a buyer for a $600,000 house. The seller agreed to pay a 6% commission on the sale to Sara's broker. Sara is on a 50-50 split with her broker. What is the amount of Sara's commission?

Solution:

Practice Problem #2

Paul, a real estate broker, listed a parcel of land for $500,000, with a commission of 10%. A few days later, he presented an offer that was 5% less than the listed price. The seller agreed to accept the price if the broker would reduce his commission by 15%. If Paul agrees to the seller's proposal, how much will his commission be?

Solution:

Interest and Loan Problems

The charge for the use of money is called **interest**. The rate of interest that is charged will determine the total dollar amount of the payments. When money is borrowed, both the principal and interest must be repaid according to the agreement between the borrower and lender.

Interest Terms	
(P) Principal:	dollar amount of money borrowed, loan amount
(I) Interest:	charge for the use of money
(R) Rate:	percentage of interest charged

Practice Problem #3

Andrea borrowed $6,000 for one year and paid $520 interest. What was the interest rate she paid?

Solution:

Practice Problem #4

If one month's interest is $50 on a five-year, interest-only note, and the interest rate on the note is 10% per year, what is the amount of the loan?

Solution:

Capitalization Problems

Capitalization problems involve these three variables:

Made = **I** Net Operating **I**ncome (NOI)

Paid = **P** Value of **P**roperty

Rate = **R** Capitalization **R**ate (Cap **R**ate)

Practice Problem #5

A duplex brings in $600 per month per unit. Gail and Kevin are interested in buying the property as an investment, and need an investment rate (capitalization rate, or cap rate) of a 10% return. What should Gail and Kevin pay for the duplex?

Solution:

Practice Problem #6

Shirley paid $900,000 for an eight-unit apartment building. The gross income is $800 per month per unit, with expenses of $4,000 annually. What capitalization rate (%) will Shirley make on her investment?

Net operating income, rather than gross income, is used to calculate a capitalization rate. Therefore, the first step is to calculate the gross income and then subtract the annual expenses to arrive at the net operating income.

You will notice on the video that the gross income was inadvertently used when solving this problem. This type of mistake is easy to make so be careful on the state exam.

[All the numbers that were used in the presentation were correct, except that at the end of the problem solving process, gross annual income of $76,800 was divided by $900,000. Instead, net operating income (NOI) of $72,800 should have been divided by $900,000.]

The next page shows the correct final step.

Correct Solution to Practice Problem #6:

Gross Income = $800 per month × 8 units = $6,400 per month × 12 months = $76,800 annual gross income.

Annual Expenses = $4,000

Net Operating Income = $76,800 – $4,000 = $72,800

Formula: R = I ÷ P

R = I ÷ P

R = $72,800 ÷ $900,000

R = **The correct answer is .081 or 8%** (not .085 or 8.5%)

Investments

Investment problems involve these three variables:

Made = **I** = Income or profit earned

Paid = **P** = Amount **P**aid or invested in the **P**roperty

Rate = **R** = **R**ate of Return or Profit

Practice Problem #7

Mitch bought a house for $145,000. The house was later sold for $165,000. What is the rate (%) of profit Mitch made on this sale?

Solution:

Cost and Selling Price Problems

This type of problem is easy to identify because you will be given a selling price and be asked to calculate the amount of profit or the cost before a profit. Sometimes determining the percentage to use can be confusing. Just remember that if a profit is made, add the % to 100%, and if a loss occurs, subtract the % from 100%.

Profit or Loss on Sales involves these three variables:

Made = **I** = **I**ncrease in value

Paid = **P** = **P**urchase price or original cost of **P**roperty

Rate = **R** = **R**ate of Return (profit or loss)

Practice Problem #8

Maria sold a rural cabin for $30,000, which allowed her to make a 20% profit. What did she pay for the property?

Solution:

Practice Problem #9

A farmer put his land on the market, wanting to net a certain amount. The real estate agent who found a buyer gave the farmer a check for $90,000 after deducting a 10% commission. What was the selling price of the farm?

Solution:

Square Footage and Area Calculations

Square footage problems are fairly simple and can be solved easily using these simple formulas.

Area = Length × Width

Length = Area ÷ Width

Width = Area ÷ Length

All buildings are not square or rectangular and therefore may be irregular in shape. Always reduce the building to squares, rectangles, and triangles and use the appropriate formula to determine the square footage.

Practice Problem #10

Fred owned four acres of land with a front footage of 500 feet along the street. What is the depth of the land?

Solution:

Practice Problem #11

Lydia and Cliff bought a lot with the intention of building a house on it. They needed to determine how much it would cost to build the house. They were told by contractors that the cost to build was $40 per square foot for a garage and $80 per square foot for a home.

Lydia and Cliff had plans drawn for the house. They used the total square footage of the house and garage to calculate the cost to build.

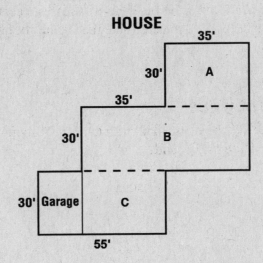

Solution:

Exam Cram Workbook - Part 2: California Portion

Getting Started

Hello, my name is Sherry Shindler Price. I'm the author of your textbook, *California Real Estate Principles*, as well as 3 others; *Real Estate Finance*, *Real Estate Practice* and *Principles and Practices of Escrow*.

I've taught real estate courses at California Community Colleges since 1986 and have developed continuing education courses and written items for state licensing exams in several states.

I hold real estate broker licenses in California as well as North Carolina, and while working as a broker specialized in multi family and other investment properties.

In your preparation to take the California State Licensing exam, you have studied national topics that are known to be included in most state exams, as well as in the California exam.

Now, welcome to the California specific portion of Allied's Exam Cram Course. In this section, we are going to discuss various California laws, disclosures, and other information you will need to know to pass the California licensing examination.

This part augments information learned in Part 1 of the California Exam Cram Course with California specific details.

California Topics

This part augments information learned in Part 1 of the California Exam Cram with California specific details.

Welcome to the California portion of Allied's Exam Cram. In this section, we are going to discuss various California laws, disclosures, and other information you will need to know to pass the California licensing examination.

Topic 1, Property, Estates & Ownership

In Topic 1, we will discuss water rights, homesteads, and community property ownership rights.

Water Rights

Water on the surface of the land or underground is real property. All water within California is the property of the State.

California Law Recognizes Surface Water and Groundwater

Surface Water

Surface water is the water found on the land in:

- ♦ watercourses—natural springs, streams, or rivers.
- ♦ bodies of water—ponds or lakes.

Surface water includes drainage water, storm water, and floodwater until it replenishes groundwater by percolating through the soil.

Groundwater

Groundwater is the water beneath the surface of the land that fills the spaces and cavities between the rocks and soil.

California's legally recognized classifications of groundwater:

- • subterranean streams
- • underflow of surface waters
- • percolating groundwater.
  - ♦ overlying land use
  - ♦ surplus groundwater

California's System of Water Rights

California's system of water rights is based on riparian rights, appropriation, percolating groundwater rights, and pueblo rights.

Riparian Rights

The owner of property bordering a surface water source (stream, river, pond, or lakes) has riparian rights. **Riparian rights** apply to surface waters flowing over, adjacent to, or standing on the property (e.g., a lake).

Surface water CANNOT be:

- owned,

- channeled, or

- dammed for the benefit of one landowner to the detriment of other property owners.

The RIPARIAN RIGHT IS not a personal right; it IS PART OF THE LAND. When riparian land is sold, the riparian right remains with the land.

Appropriative Water Rights

An **appropriative water right** is the right to take riparian surface water for a beneficial use on non-adjacent property.

Beneficial Uses of Water
- Domestic purposes

- Irrigation

- Fire protection

- Mining

- Watering stock

- Sprinkling to protect crops from heat or frost damage

- Recreation

- Industrial

- Wildlife protection

- Power generation

Appropriative Water Rights:

- are obtained from California Water Resources Control Board.

- can be held by any legal entity—individuals, trusts, corporations, agencies.

- are considered real property.

- can be held together or separately from the land on which the water is used or diverted.

- can be transferred temporarily or permanently from one owner to another.

Percolating Groundwater Rights

Under the **doctrine of correlative rights**, landowners overlying percolating groundwater, such as an aquifer, may use the water on an equal and correlative basis.

Each owner is treated as having an equal right to groundwater regardless of when first use was initiated.

Overlying rights are similar to riparian rights and the landowners do not have to obtain a permit to use their percolating groundwater.

Pueblo Rights

Pueblo rights, which are derived from Spanish law, give pueblos the right to claim surface water and groundwater under the town. Today, water use under a pueblo right is limited to ordinary municipal purposes that occur within city limits.

Dower and Curtesy Rights

The common law concept—*dower* and *curtesy*—deals with the inheritance of the husband and wife from each other.

California uses COMMUNITY PROPERTY and JOINT TENANCY combined with the LAWS OF DESCENT AND DISTRIBUTION to protect a surviving spouse's interest in marital property.

Homestead

California homestead laws protect the family home. A **homestead property** is the home (primary residence) occupied by a family that is exempt from the claims of, or eviction by, unsecured creditors.

Homestead Exemption

A **homestead exemption** is a lien that protects a certain amount of equity in a person's home by limiting the amount of liability for certain debts against which a home can be used to satisfy a judgment.

A homestead exemption does NOT STOP the sale of the property.

A homestead exemption ensures that the homeowner receives the amount of the exemption before the creditors are paid from the sale proceeds.

Two homestead exemptions in California—automatic and declared.

Automatic Homestead

The **automatic homestead (statutory homestead exemption)** is automatic and only applies on the forced sale of the property.

Because it is automatic:

- anyone living in his or her home has an automatic homestead exemption protecting the equity.

- a declaration of homestead does NOT need to be filed.

The homeowner must live continuously on the property from the date the judgment creditor's lien attaches until the date the court determines that the dwelling is a homestead. A **dwelling** is the place where a person resides.

Declared Homestead

A **declared homestead** is the dwelling described in a homestead declaration.

A Declaration of Homestead:

- is a recorded notice a property owner files to protect the equity in his or her real property.

- PROTECTS real estate dwellings.

- does NOT PROTECT personal property dwellings such as mobilehomes on leased land, houseboats, or other waterborne vessels.

Requirements for a Declaration of Homestead to Create a Homestead

- Name of the declared homestead owner.

- Description of the declared homestead.

- Statement that the declared homestead is the principal dwelling of the declared homestead owner.

- The declaration of homestead must be signed, acknowledged, and recorded to take effect.

- Once the declaration of homestead is recorded, the property becomes a homestead.

A Declared Homestead can be Terminated:

- by recording a **notice of abandonment**,

- by conveying the property, or

- through an execution and forced sale.

An owner must file an **Abandonment of Homestead** form in order to obtain a homestead on a new property. If the owner moves from the homesteaded property and does not wish to file a new declaration of homestead, the original homestead remains valid.

Sale of the property automatically causes the homestead to terminate. However, neither death of the homesteader nor destruction of the property terminates the homestead.

Community Property

California is a community property state. **Community property** is all property acquired by a married person while living with a spouse during a valid marriage—except for certain separate property.

Property Excluded from Community Property Treatment

- Property owned before marriage.

- Property acquired by either spouse during marriage by gift or inheritance.

- Income derived from separate property.

Community property cannot be sold or encumbered by only one of the partners.

Either spouse may lease community property for **up to one year** or may sign a listing agreement to put a property on the market.

A listing agreement signed by only one spouse is enforceable.

However, both must accept and sign any contract to actually sell the community property.

Either spouse may buy real or personal property without the consent of the other. Both are bound by the contract made by either one, unless the new property is bought specifically as separate property with funds from a separate property account.

Intestate Sucession Rules in Community Property

When vesting is community property, if there is no will, the surviving spouse inherits all community property by **intestate succession**.

Regarding separate property, if there is no will, the surviving spouse gets one-half and one child gets one-half.

If there is more than one child, the surviving spouse gets one-third and the children get two-thirds.

How Married Couples Take Title in California

A married couple in California has three choices when it comes to how they may take title—joint tenancy, community property, community property with the right of survivorship.

In California, married persons **do not take title** in tenancy by the entirety. Unless otherwise stated, title is presumed community property.

The first type of vesting is **joint tenancy**, which includes the right of survivorship if one of the spouses dies, which may also include a tax liability for the surviving spouse.

The second type of vesting is **community property**, which does not include the right of survivorship, but also includes probate after a spouse dies and all the costs involved in that process.

The third type of vesting is **community property with the right of survivorship**, which includes the better of the first two types of vesting. There is no particular tax liability because of the death of a spouse and there is no probate with its seemingly endless costs.

Topic 1, Property, Estates & Ownership - Review
Multiple-Choice Questions

1. A running stream is considered:
    a. personal property.
    b. real property.
    c. a fixture.
    d. a chattel.

2. Water found on the land in watercourses, such as natural springs, streams, or rivers and in bodies of water, such as ponds or lakes is called:
    a. drainage water.
    b. groundwater.
    c. surface water.
    d. waste water.

3. Which of the following statements concerning riparian rights is not correct?
    a. Riparian property owners have reasonable use of flowing water.
    b. The owner of property bordering a stream or river has riparian rights.
    c. Riparian property owners own the water and may use it.
    d. The owner of adjacent land may not lawfully divert all available waterand thereby deprive a riparian owner of water.

4. When the state has given permission to a non-riparian rights owner of a farm to use a nearby lake, the owner has received this right by:
    a. appropriation.
    b. eminent domain.
    c. estoppel.
    d. percolation.

5. The right to use any water controlled by the state rather than by the landowner adjacent to the water is called:
    a. avulsion.
    b. littoral rights.
    c. prior appropriation.
    d. riparian rights.

6. Because California is a community property state, a surviving spouse does not need to deal with the common law concept of:
    a. caveat emptor.
    b. dower and curtesy.
    c. escheat.
    d. eminent domain.

7. There are certain requirements for a valid Declaration of Homestead. All of the following are requirements of the law, except:
    a. a verification as to the cost of the property when purchased.
    b. name of the declared homestead owner
    c. description of the declared homestead
    d. statement that the declared homestead is the principal dwelling of the declared homestead owner.

8. A declared homestead can be terminated:
    a. by recording a notice of abandonment
    b. by conveying the property
    c. through a forced sale
    d. in all of the ways mentioned in the previous choices.

9. A declared homestead is terminated by:
    a. destruction of the property.
    b. selling the property.
    c. death of the homesteader.
    d. all of the above.

10. To be valid, which of the following must be recorded?
    a. Easement
    b. Contract for sale
    c. Homestead
    d. Lease

11. As a real estate licensee, you will often be asked to explain a Declaration of Homestead. All of the following are correct statements concerning this protection, except:
    a. it does not protect the homeowner against mechanic's liens, tax liens, deeds of trust, or mortgages.
    b. it may be declared on a resident-owner 21-unit apartment house.
    c. it may be declared on only one property of an individual; however, upon sale of the property and purchase of a new property a declaration may be recorded on the new property without a formal Declaration of Abandonment of the first Declaration of Homestead.
    d. a declaration is not valid unless recorded prior to the filing of a court action.

12. A contract to sell community real property made by one spouse only is:
    a. valid.
    b. illegal.
    c. enforceable.
    d. unenforceable.

13. A man and wife have title to real property vested as John Jones and his wife Mary. This method of taking title would mean:
    a. the wife may not will her undivided 1/2 interest in the property.
    b. a presumption that the property is held as joint tenants.
    c. a presumption that title is held as tenants in common but without the right to will their interest by either spouse.
    d. a presumption that title is vested as community property and either spouse may will his interest to whomever he chooses; however, if either spouse dies intestate the surviving spouse would inherit the deceased spouse's interest without probate.

14. A spouse may lease real community property without the other spouse's consent:
    a. if the property is in his name.
    b. for up to one year.
    c. because he is the statutory manager of the community property.
    d. if the lease is oral.

15. A spouse can will:
    a. all of the community property.
    b. 1/2 of the community property.
    c. any community property the other spouse has not willed.
    d. none of the community property.

16. An 18-year-old wife bought property with her separate funds and instructed escrow to vest title in her 17-year- old husband and herself as community property. The purchase contract was:
    a. valid.
    b. void.
    c. voidable.
    d. unenforceable.

Answer Key

1. (b) Water on the surface, flowing in a stream or underground (percolating) is real property. If it is taken and bottled, then it becomes personal.

2. (c) California recognizes two sources of water—surface water and groundwater. Surface water is the water found on the land in watercourses, such as natural springs, streams, or rivers and in bodies of water, such as ponds or lakes.

3. (c) The owner of property bordering a stream or river has riparian rights. Riparian property owners have reasonable use of flowing water, providing it does not injure other riparian landowners.

4. (a) An appropriative water right is the right to take riparian surface water for a beneficial use on non-adjacent property. California policy is that the use of water for domestic purposes is the highest use of water and that the next highest use is for irrigation.

5. (c) The right to use any water, with the exception of limited domestic use, is controlled by the the State of California Water Resources Control Board rather than the landowner adjacent to the water, is called prior appropriation.

6. (b) In California the use of community property and joint tenancies and the laws of descent and distribution have made it unnecessary to use dower and curtesy.

7. (a) When declaring a homestead, it is not necessary to divulge the purchase price.

8. (d) A homestead can be terminated by recording a notice of abandonment, by conveying the property, or through an execution and forced sale.

9. (b) Neither death of the homesteader nor destruction of the property terminates the homestead.

10. (c) The declaration of homestead must be signed, acknowledged, and recorded to take effect.

11. (d) A Declaration of Homestead is the recorded document that protects a homeowner from foreclosure by certain judgment creditors. It can be filed after the filing of a court action but must be filed before the filing of a judgment.

12. (d) A contract to sell community real property must be signed by both spouses. If it is signed by only one, the contract cannot be enforced.

13. (d) Property vested as John Jones and his wife Mary, unless otherwise stated, is presumed to be community property.

14. (b) If for more than one year, one spouse must have the other spouse's consent.

15. (b) Either spouse has the right to will 1/2 the community property.

16. (a) If the purchaser has legal capacity the sale is valid. In whom the title is vested does not affect the legality of the sale. The title could vest in a 3-year-old child.

Topic 2, Encumbrances & Transfer of Ownership

In Topic 2, we will discuss encumbrances, easements, encroachments, and transfer of ownership.

Encumbrances

An **encumbrance** is a non-possessory interest in real property that is held by someone who is not the owner.

Anything that burdens or affects the title or the use of the property is an encumbrance.

Two Types of Encumbrances

- Those that affect the title are known as financial encumbrances.

- Those that affect the use of the property are known as non-financial encumbrances.

Easement -A Non-Financial Encumbrance

An **easement** is the right to enter or use someone else's land for a specified purpose.

An interest in an easement is **non-possessory**.

That means the holder of an easement can use it only for the purpose intended and may not exclude anyone else from using it.

Easement by Necessity

In California, an **easement by necessity** can only be recognized when one parcel has been created out of another, and the resulting parcel would be completely inaccessible without access across the "parent" parcel from which it was created.

If a parcel has legal access to a public roadway, even if it is circuitous and inconvenient (e.g., crossing an unpaved hill when a public road could be reached across a shorter path), then an easement by necessity cannot be created because it is not, in fact, a necessity.

An easement by necessity is automatically terminated when another ingress/egress becomes available.

Easement by Prescription

An **easement by prescription** allows someone to acquire an interest in a property, not actual ownership, after certain requirements are met.

Creating an Easement by Prescription

- Continuous and uninterrupted use, by a single party

- For a period of 5 years.

- Use must be against the owner's wishes

- Use must be open and notorious

- Some reasonable claim to use of the property

Encroachments

An **encroachment** is the intrusion into, under, or over the property of another without that person's permission.

In California, the statute of limitations to remove an encroachment is 3 years after discovery of the encroachment, or the improvements will be allowed to remain.

When property is transferred in California, a survey is not required. Therefore, disputes regarding boundary encroachments are common.

Encroachment disputes typically involve:
- buildings
- fences
- driveways
- landscaping

Transfer of Ownership

Real property may be acquired and conveyed by will, succession, accession, adverse possession, and transfer.

Will

California recognizes three types of wills: witnessed wills, statutory form wills, and holographic wills.

Witnessed Will

A **witnessed will**, usually prepared by an attorney, is signed by the maker (testator) and is witnessed by at least two persons.

Requirements for a Witnessed Will

- In writing
- Signed by the testator or signed by someone else in the testator's presence, and at the testator's direction
- Witnessed by at least two persons each of whom:
  - was present at the same time, witnessed either the signing of the will or the testator's acknowledgment of the signature or of the will, and
  - understand that the instrument they sign is the testator's will.

Testator's Signature on a Will. The testator's signature on the will is sometimes referred to as the testator's **authentication** of the will.

At one time, a testator who could not read or write could make a **signature by "mark"**. Today, someone other than the testator can sign the will if the testator is physically unable to sign the will, e.g., blind, too infirm, etc. The person acting for the testator must sign the will in the testator's presence and at the testator's direction.

Statutory Form Will

Any person over the age of 18 and of sound mind may execute a **statutory form will**.

A statutory will still requires two witnesses and can be amended by **codicil** or revoked in the same manner as other wills.

Holographic Wills

A **holographic will** is a will entirely in the handwriting of the testator.

However, a holographic will may be a combination of the testator's own handwriting part of a commercially printed form will.

Unlike a regular will, a holographic will does not require witnesses.

Succession

Succession is the legal transfer of a person's interests in real and personal property under the **laws of descent and distribution**. Succession is largely governed in California by the Probate Code.

The decedent is referred to as "**an intestate**" and is said to "**die intestate**". The law of **intestate succession** is what governs the transfer of property from a decedent to an heir when the decedent fails to dispose of the property by will.

If there is a surviving spouse, that spouse is entitled to a one-half share of the community property.

The decedent's separate property (i.e., non-community property) is governed by a series of "either/or" provisions, depending upon whether the intestate decedent left a surviving spouse only or a surviving spouse and children—and if neither of those, other relatives according to degree.

The following chart shows these possibilities with regard to the separate property.

DISTRIBUTION	
Surviving spouse (only)	All separate property
Surviving spouse and one child	One-half to surviving spouse/ one half to child
Surviving spouse and a parent (or parents)	One-half to surviving spouse/ one half to parent(s)
Surviving spouse and two or more children or one child and the "issue" (descendants) of any deceased child or children	One-third to surviving spouse/ two-thirds to children

If there is no surviving spouse, the property is divided into as many equal shares as there are living members of the nearest generation of issue. **Issue** means descendants of the testator.

If there are still no surviving relatives, then the property can pass to the **next of kin**—nearest blood relatives of the decedent who do not fall into one of the earlier categories.

If no one meets those requirements, it can then be distributed to the parents or other close relatives of a predeceased spouse.

If no surviving relatives are found, the property escheats to the State, which holds it in trust until someone who can show that they are entitled to the property comes forward.

Adverse Possession

In California, actual ownership of real property can be acquired by **adverse possession**.

The requirements for adverse possession are the same as for easement by prescription with the additional requirement of payment of taxes.

Requirements to Acquire Ownership through Adverse Possession

- Open possession (some assertion of control, such as fencing or use)

- Notorious possession (i.e., such as a reasonable owner of the property would otherwise recognize)

- Continuous for a 5-year time period

- Pay property taxes on the disputed property for the entire 5 years of the disputed claim.

- Hostile (not with the original owner's permission)

- Adverse to a claim of right (adverse possessor must claim the title)

In addition, the adverse possessor will have to file a lawsuit to **quiet title** against the person who, until that point, had valid title to the property.

Lawsuit to quiet title is necessary to extinquish ownership rights of owner of record.

Transfer

Property is acquired by **transfer** when, by an act of the parties or law, title is **conveyed**, or transferred, from one person to another by means of a written document.

The transfer may be:

- **voluntary**, such as the sale of a home, or

- **involuntary by act of law**, such as a foreclosure sale.

Ways to Transfer (Alienate) Real Property

- Private grant

- Public grant

- Public dedication

- Operation of law (**court action**)

Types of Deeds

Different states and local jurisdictions have differing requirements for the types of deeds that may be used when conveying real property interests, including differing requirements for the form and presentation of the deed.

The kinds of deeds commonly used to transfer ownership include warranty deeds, bargain and sale deeds, grant deeds, and quitclaim deeds.

Warranty deeds are used all over the United States and are the most commonly used deed in Texas.

Grant deeds are used in some states and **are the most commonly used deed in California**.

Grant Deed

In California, the **grant deed** is the most frequently used instrument to transfer title. The parties to the grant deed are the **grantor** and **grantee**.

A grant deed must have a **granting clause** as well as two **implied warranties** by the grantor.
1. The grantor has not already conveyed title to any other person, and

2. The estate is free from encumbrances other than those disclosed by the grantor.

Requirements for a Valid Grant Deed

- According to the statute of frauds, a **deed must be in writing**.

- The grantor must be competent to convey the property (not a minor or incompetent).

- The property must be adequately described but it does not require a legal description.

- Words of granting such as grant or convey must be included.

- The deed must be executed (signed) by the grantor. The deed may be signed by a witnessed mark "X".

- The deed must be delivered to and accepted by the grantee.

Items a Valid Deed in California Does NOT Require

- Acknowledgment & Recording

- Competent grantee; may be a minor, felon or incompetent

- Date

- Mention of the consideration

- Signature of grantee

- Habendum clause. Deeds no longer require language known as the **habendum clause** (also known as the "have and to hold" clause).

- Seal or witnesses

- Legal description. In California, it is NOT a requirement for a deed to use a legal description. The real property must be adequately described so that it is clear which parcel of land is being conveyed. However, as a practical matter it is better to use a legal description that identifies the parcel more specifically, such as a metes and bounds description or by reference to a recorded plat map.

Topic 2, Encumbrances & Transfer of Ownership - Review

Multiple-Choice Questions

1. Which of the following is the best definition of encumbrance?
   a. The degree, quantity, and extent of interest a person has in real property.
   b. Anything that affects or limits the fee simple title to or value of property.
   c. The use of property as security for a debt.
   d. Any action regarding property, other than acquiring or transferring   title.

2. An interest in real property may be acquired by either prescription or by adverse possession. The interest resulting from prescription is:
   a. the right to use another's land.
   b. a possessory title.
   c. an equitable interest.
   d. a private grant.

3. Prescription is a method of acquiring which of the following?
   a. Medical drugs from a pharmacist
   b. Easements
   c. Utility rights
   d. None of the above

4. If a building extends beyond the land of its owner and covers some land of an adjoining property, what is created?
   a. An encumbrance
   b. An encroachment
   c. An easement
   d. A prescriptive easement

5. After purchasing a home, Mr. Brown discovered that his neighbor's fence was 2 feet over the line on his property. His legal remedy is to bring a civil suit against:
   a. the title company from which he had purchased a standard policy of title insurance.
   b. his neighbor, under the law of adverse possession.
   c. the broker for failure to disclose the encroachment.
   d. his neighbor, for removal of the encroachment on grounds of trespass.

6. Tenants, Bob and Lisa Jones, allowed the children from the neighboring back lot to enter a gate in their backyard and travel through to the front yard in order to catch their school bus every weekday. By doing this, what have they created?
   a. An encroachment
   b. A leasehold estate
   c. A less-than-freehold estate
   d. A license

7. Which of the following wills is not recognized in California?
   a. Holographic will
   b. Nuncupative will
   c. Statutory form will
   d. Witnessed will

8. A married man died without leaving a witnessed will. However, after his death, his wife found a statement naming his son as executor and expressing his wishes for the disposition of his estate. It was dated three years previously and was entirely written and signed by him in pencil. This would mean:
   a. an administrator would be appointed to preserve his estate until the completion of probate.
   b. he died intestate and his wife would be executrix of the estate.
   c. his will would be classified as nuncupative and his wife would receive his estate without probate.
   d. his death would be classified as testate; however, any real property would have to be probated in whatever state it is located.

9. The requirements for a witnessed will do not require that the:
   a. testator signs the will.
   b. will is witnessed by at least two witnesses.
   c. testator signs the will in the presence of the witnesses.
   d. will is in writing.

10. At one time, a testator who could not read or write could sign the will by making a signature by "mark". Today, if a person is physically unable to sign the will:
    a. the law allows someone other than the testator to sign the will.
    b. the law requires a blood relative to sign the will for the testator.
    c. a person is precluded from making a will.
    d. an interested party may help the testator make a video will.

11. Which statement is true regarding holographic wills?
    a.   A holographic will is prepared wholly by an attorney.
    b.   A holographic will is in the handwriting of the testator.
    c.   A holographic will requires witnesses.
    d.   A holographic will must be dated.

12. In California, title to real property can be transferred in all of the following ways, except:
    a.   by deed.
    b.   by accession.
    c.   by sufferance.
    d.   by succession

13. Prescription is a method of acquiring an easement. Adverse possession is a method of acquiring title. Which of the following statements is correct?
    a.   Dedication of land for use by the public could result in creating an easement by prescription.
    b.   In a claim of title by adverse possession, establishing residence on the property would be a necessary element.
    c.   Granting grazing rights in excess of five years on agricultural land could result in prescriptive rights to an easement.
    d.   None of the above statements is correct.

14. Which of the following statements best matches the term alienation?
    a.   Contract of leasing
    b.   Contract of conveyance
    c.   Contract of money
    d.   Contract of pledge

15. When no relatives can be found to whom a deceased person has left property in a will or when the person has died without a will, which term is used to describe the transfer of the property to the State of California?
    a.   Ademption
    b.   Codicil
    c.   Escheat
    d.   Testamentary

Answer Key

1. (b) This is the Bureau of Real Estate's (new name for DRE) definition of an encumbrance.

2. (a) Prescription (easement by prescription) only conveys the right to use another's land.

3. (b) Easements may be created in many ways. Prescription is one method of creating easements.

4. (b) If a permanent improvement such as a fence, wall, driveway, or roof extends over the lot line into adjacent property owned by another person, it is known as an encroachment.

5. (d) Encroachment is a form of trespass and actionable in law.

6. (d) A license is the permission to use property that can be revoked at any time. It can be granted by a tenant as long as it does not conflict the terms of the lease.

7. (b) California recognizes three types of wills: witnessed wills, statutory form wills, and holographic wills. A nuncupative (oral) will is spoken rather than dictated or written. It is not valid in California and only recognized in very few states, and only under exceptional circumstances like an impending death of a soldier in a foreign land.

8. (d) A handwritten unwitnessed will is a holographic will and is legal. Real property is always probated in the state where located.

9. (c) A witnessed will must be in writing, signed by the testator, and witnessed by at least two witnesses. However, the testator does not need to sign the will in the presence of the two witnesses.

10. (a) Today, §6110 allows someone other than the testator to sign the will (physically) if, e.g., the testator is blind, too infirm, etc. This provision requires that the person acting for the testator sign the will in the testator's presence and at the testator's direction. Video recordings are not valid wills in the state of California. Like an oral will, this could be done in those cases where time is of essence like in the case of a dying person. It could be admitted in the court only as a supportive tool of a written will, and not individually and that too only in extraordinary circumstances.

11. (b) A holographic will is a will entirely in the handwriting of the testator.

12. (c) Real property may be acquired or conveyed in the following ways: will, succession, accession, occupancy, and transfer of deed.

13. (d) Answer (a) would be an easement by statutory dedication. In adverse possession, it is not necessary to establish residence, only to hold and occupy the land continuously for five years. In an easement by prescription, the user of the property must be hostile to the owner. In answer (c) the owner is giving permission to use the property.

14. (b) Property is acquired by transfer when, by an act of the parties or law, title is conveyed, or transferred. Real property may be transferred, or alienated by private grant, public grant, public dedication, or operation of law (a court action).

15. (c) If no surviving relatives are found, the property escheats to the State, which holds it in trust until someone who can show that they are entitled to the property comes forward.

Topic 3, Contracts: The Basics

In Topic 3, we will discuss express contracts and the statutes of fraud and limitations.

Contract Classifications

Express contract – the parties declare the terms and put their intentions in words, oral or written.

> Example – Rental Agreement. As a valid contract, a rental agreement must have the same components as a legally enforceable contract—legally competent parties, mutual consent between the parties, a lawful objective, and sufficient consideration. The rental agreement is not only a contract; it is also a conveyance of a leasehold interest in real estate, which gives the renter a tenancy.

Rental agreements **FOR ONE YEAR OR LESS** can be oral or in writing.

Leases **FOR LONGER THAN ONE YEAR** (**1 year plus 1 day**) must be in writing.

However, all rental agreements should be in writing to clarify the duties and responsibilities of each party and reduce disagreements.

Statute of Frauds

Most contracts required by law to be in writing are under the **statute of frauds**. This is to prevent fraud in the sale of land or an interest in land.

Contracts That Must Be in Writing

- An agreement for the sale of real property (e.g., *offers and acceptances, deeds, land contracts, options to purchase, escrows*)

- An agreement that cannot be performed within a year from its making. (e.g., *leases for more than one year*)

- An agreement to employ an agent, broker, or other person to purchase, sell, or to lease real estate for longer than one year, for compensation or a commission (e.g., *listing agreements, buyer representation agreements*)

- An agreement by a purchaser of real property to pay an indebtedness secured by a mortgage or deed of trust upon the property purchased, unless the purchaser's assumption of the indebtedness is provided for in the conveyance of the property (e.g., *trust deeds and promissory notes, loan assumptions*)

Statute of Limitations

The **statute of limitations** places a limit on the length of time a plaintiff has to file a lawsuit.

Once the statute of limitations has expired, any lawsuit that could have been brought to enforce one's contractual rights is terminated just as completely as if they had not existed in the first place.

Time Limits for Filing Civil Actions

90 Days Civil actions to recover personal property such as suitcases, clothing, or jewelry alleged to have been left at a hotel or in an apartment; must begin within 90 days after the owners depart from the personal property.

6 Months Action against an officer to recover property seized in an official capacity—such as by a tax collector.

1 Year Libel or slander, injury or death caused by wrongful act, or loss to depositor against a bank for the payment of a forged check.

2 Years Action on a contract, **not in writing**; action based on a policy of title insurance.

3 Years Action on a liability created by statute; action for trespass on or injury to real property (e.g., encroachment); action for relief on the grounds of fraud or mistake; attachment.

4 Years Action on any written contract; includes most real estate contracts.

10 Years Action on a judgment or decree of any court in the United States.

Topic 3, Contracts: The Basics - Review
Multiple-Choice Questions

1. Mr. Miller made an express written offer to purchase a home through broker Cook. However, Miller died in a car accident before broker Cook could notify him of an unqualified, signed acceptance by the seller. Which of the following statements is most correct?
   a. The death of Miller constituted a revocation of the offer.
   b. The acceptance does not have to be communicated to the buyer.
   c. Notification of acceptance to the executor would bind the Miller estate.
   d. The contract would not be binding because the deed had not been delivered into escrow.

2. Of the following, which is most correct concerning the statute of frauds?
   a. Misrepresentation in the making of a contract violates the statute.
   b. It classifies most oral real estate contracts as unenforceable.
   c. It classifies an oral agreement between brokers to share a commission as unenforceable.
   d. Violations of this statute are prosecuted by the district attorney in the county where the alleged violation occurred.

3. Broker Fisher secured an agency listing in writing from the Walker Co. on a commercial building that had been vacant for some months. The listing broker entered into an oral agreement to share his commission with a cooperating broker. The cooperating broker procured a buyer, but broker Fisher refused to split the commission. The cooperating broker:
   a. may recover his share in court.
   b. may not recover his share in court because this was only an oral agreement.
   c. should ask the Commissioner to arbitrate the dispute.
   d. should go to the Labor Commissioner.

4. The statute of frauds requires that all of the following contracts must be a record in writing to be enforceable except a(n):
   a. agreement allowing a broker to sell real estate for compensation.
   b. lease agreement of one year to commence one month after date of execution.
   c. agreement to sell land.
   d. agreement between two brokers to split a commission.

5. The statute of frauds requires which of the following contracts to be in writing?
    a. An employment contract to represent the seller of a business opportunity
    b. A contract selling a business opportunity
    c. A contract that is not to be performed within one year of its making
    d. A nine-month lease

6. A buyer must bring a lawsuit for breach of written contract against a seller within:
    a. 6 months.
    b. 1 year.
    c. 3 years.
    d. 4 years.

7. Four months ago seller Snow accepted an offer from buyer Bell to purchase her home. The contract was in writing. Later, Snow refused to complete the transaction. Under the Statute of limitations Bell must file an action within:
    a. 2 years.
    b. 3 years.
    c. 4 years.
    d. 5 years.

8. Within how many years must a buyer bring a lawsuit for breach of an oral agreement against the broker?
    a. 1 year
    b. 2 years
    c. 3 years
    d. 4 years

Answer Key

1. (a) Death of the offeror constitutes a revocation of the offer. Legally, if the acceptance had been communicated to buyer before the accident, the contract would have been binding on his estate.

2. (b) The statute of frauds states that contracts must be in writing to be enforceable. Its main function is for the prevention of fraud.

3. (a) The statute of frauds does not require an agreement between brokers to split a commission to be in writing to be enforceable. If the cooperating broker can prove his case, he can recover his share in court.

4. (d) An oral agreement to split a commission is enforceable at law.

5. (c) A contract that is not to be performed within one year of its making must be in writing in order to be enforceable under the statute of frauds.

6. (d) The Statute of limitations requires lawsuits for breach of a written contract to be filed within four years of the breach.

7. (c) Statute of limitations on any written contract is 4 years.

8. (b) The Statute of limitations requires lawsuits for breach of an oral agreement to be filed within two years of the breach.

Topic 4, Agency Relationships

In Topic 4, we will discuss disclosing the agency relationship, listing agreements, and buyer representation agreements.

In California, every agency relationship has a principal, an agent, and a third party. They are bound together in a legal relationship, with all the duties and rights that go with that connection.

Parties in a Real Estate Agency Relationship

- **Principal** (buyer or seller)

- **Agent** (real estate broker)

- **Third party** (customer)

Sellers employ **listing agents** to find buyers for their properties.

Buyers often employ **buyer's agents** to locate properties.

Because the listing and buyer agents represent their principals, they are in a **single agency**.

California allows **dual agency** in a transaction, but the broker must have the informed, written consent of both the seller and the buyer.

California does not recognize designated agency or transactional agency.

Disclosing the Agency Relationship

The **Agency Relationship Disclosure Act** applies to every residential property transaction of 1-to-4 units. It requires that an agent give a written Disclosure Regarding Real Estate Agency Relationships document to sellers and/or buyers explaining the nature of agency. This disclosure must be made PRIOR to taking a listing or writing an offer.

The steps in the disclosure process are disclose the relationship, elect the agency, and confirm the agency.

Steps in the Disclosure Process
Disclose

Elect

Confirm

Listing and Buyer Representation Agreements

Listing and **buyer representation agreements** are written bilateral (or unilateral) employment contracts by which a principal (seller or buyer) employs a broker to sell real estate.

An exclusive authorization and right to sell listing agreement is a **bilateral contract**—in that a promise is given in exchange for a promise.

Topic 4, Agency Relationships - Review
Multiple-Choice Questions

1. Every agency relationship has a principal, an agent, and a third party. In a real estate transaction, the agent is the:
    a. buyer.
    b. seller.
    c. broker.
    d. customer.

2. If a listing broker acts as an agent, the broker owes to the seller a fiduciary duty. What does the broker owe to the buyer?
    a. The same fiduciary duty
    b. A duty of fair and honest dealing
    c. A duty to answer all questions
    d. A duty to disclose all information regarding the selling price only

3. The person who gives authority to an agent to represent his or her interests in dealing with a third party is the:
    a. client.
    b. Real Estate Commissioner.
    c. principal.
    d. escrow agent.

4. Which of the following is true of a buyer's agent?
    a. They are illegal in California
    b. They are not entitled to a commission
    c. They do not form an agency relationship
    d. Compensation may not necessarily come from the buyer

5. Which of the following types of agency representation is allowed in California?
   a. Appointed agency
   b. Designated agency
   c. Dual agency
   d. Transactional agency

6. Which of the following is not required of a licensee under the current agency disclosure law?
   a. Disclosure
   b. Election
   c. Confirmation
   d. Representation

7. Which of the following forms must be completed before an offer can be written?
   a. Agency disclosure
   b. Deposit receipt
   c. Real estate transfer disclosure
   d. Listing

8. Agency is referred to as the relationship between the agent and his or her principal. All of the following statements are correct about agency, except:
   a. agency may be an expressed contract.
   b. the principal must pay money to the agent to create an agency relationship.
   c. agency may be an implied contract.
   d. an agency agreement may be in writing or oral.

9. A bilateral contract is one that is a(n):
   a. promise for performance.
   b. promise for an act.
   c. act for a promise.
   d. promise for a promise.

10. An exclusive authorization and right to sell listing just entered into can be described as:
    a. a cash agreement to purchase properties that are bilateral.
    b. a bilateral executory contract.
    c. a land contract whereby licensee may obtain commissions from both the buyer and seller.
    d. all of the above.

11. A new contract between the seller of real property and a licensee whereby the seller agrees to pay the licensee a commission if he produces a ready, willing, and able buyer and the licensee agrees to use due diligence in procuring a buyer, is called:

    a.   unilateral executory contract.

    b.   bilateral executory contract.

    c.   unilateral executed contract.

    d.   bilateral executed contract.

12. A husband and wife owned their home as joint tenants. The husband signed an exclusive authorization and right to sell listing agreement with a broker without disclosing the manner of title holding in the property and without his wife's signature on the listing. In the event of a commission dispute, the broker:

    a.   may bring action to force the wife to sell her interest.

    b.   may sue the husband separately in civil court for his commission.

    c.   has no right to a commission because he failed to obtain the wife's signature on the listing.

    d.   may bring court action against the community estate.

13. In a real estate contract, the promise to use due diligence is made by whom?

    a.   The buyer

    b.   The seller

    c.   The escrow agent

    d.   The listing broker

14. Listing agreements may be recorded at the county recorder's office by:

    a.   listing brokers.

    b.   sellers.

    c.   escrow companies.

    d.   none of the above.

15. In the preparation of an exclusive right to represent buyer contract, a licensee may be disciplined if he or she fails to include:

    a.   the asking terms of the financing.

    b.   a clause making the agreement bilateral.

    c.   a clause indicating that time is of the essence in carrying out the terms of the contract.

    d.   a definite expiration date.

Answer Key

1. (c) Every agency relationship has a principal, an agent, and a third party. In a real estate transaction the principal (buyer or seller), agent (real estate broker), and third party (customer) are bound together in a legal relationship, with all the duties and rights that go with that connection.

2. (b) A listing broker has the duty of fair and honest dealings with third parties—the buyer. This duty includes full disclosure of all material facts.

3. (c) A principal is one of the main parties to a transaction (i.e. the buyer and the seller are principals in the purchase of real property). In a fiduciary relationship, the person who hires a real estate broker to represent him or her in the sale of property is a principal.

4. (d) Most often commissions are distributed through listing agreement with seller.

5. (c) California allows dual agency in a transaction, but the broker must have the informed, written consent of both the seller and the buyer. California does not recognize designated agency or transactional agency.

6. (d) The three steps required under the agency disclosure law are: disclose, elect, and confirm.

7. (a) The law requires that an agent supply a written document, called Disclosure Regarding Real Estate Agency Relationships, explaining the nature of agency. This disclosure must be made prior to taking a listing or writing an offer.

8. (b) Answers (a), (c), and (d) are correct statements applicable to an agency relationship. Answer (b) is false. An agency relationship does not require the payment of money.

9. (d) A bilateral (two-sided) agreement contains a promise for a promise. For example, an exclusive authorization and right to sell listing (a bilateral agreement) contains the owner's promise to pay a commission if the property sells during the listing period. In exchange for this promise, the broker promises to use due diligence in procuring a buyer for the property.

10. (b) The exclusive right to sell listing is a bilateral contract. An executory contract is one that has not been completely performed.

11. (b) A bilateral contract is a contract between two parties with each promising to act (a promise for a promise). An executory contract is a contract yet to be performed. This type of contract is a bilateral executory contract. An executed contract is one that has been completed.

12. (d) The husband binds the community estate when he fails to disclose the joint tenancy holding.

13. (d) The seller signs a listing agreement promising payment for service by the listing broker and the broker promises to use due diligence in finding a buyer - a bilateral contract in that a promise is given in exchange for a promise.

14. (d) Listings cannot be recorded whether or not notarized.

15. (d) All exclusive listings must have a definite termination date.

Topic 5, Real Estate Contracts

In Topic 5, there is no Calfornia-specific content.

Topic 6, Disclosures in Real Estate

In Topic 6, we will discuss the various disclosures required in a real estate transaction—Transfer Disclosure Statement, Mello-Roos Assessment Disclosure, Natural Hazard Disclosure Statement, Furnishing Controlling Documents, Stigmatized Property, Notice of Supplemental Property Tax Bill, Disclosure of Sales Price Information, and the Notice of Negotiability of Commissions.

Additionally, several health and energy-saving disclosures are required—such as those concerning water heaters, smoke detectors, carbon monoxide detectors, water-conserving fixtures, home energy rating, energy conservation retrofit, and thermal insulation.

Transfer Disclosure Statement

Under California law, a seller of a residential property (1-to-4 units) must deliver a written Real Estate Transfer Disclosure Statement (TDS) about the condition of the property to the prospective buyer.

The **Real Estate Transfer Disclosure Statement** (TDS) is a detailed statement telling what the seller knows about the condition of the property. The seller must list all known defects as well as any potential problems on the TDS that might affect the property value.

Usually a broker obtains the TDS at the time he or she takes a listing and gives the buyer a copy before an offer to purchase the property is presented or contract is executed.

If the disclosure statement is given to the buyer after the offer to purchase the property is presented, the buyer may terminate the contract by written notice to the seller within 3 days after receiving the disclosure statement.

The seller reveals any information that would be important to the buyer regarding the condition of the property in the TDS, and states that—to the seller's knowledge—everything important has been disclosed. Many facts about a residential property could materially affect its value and desirability.

Material Facts Affecting Desirability and Value of a Property

- Age, condition, and any defects or malfunctions of the structural components and/or plumbing, electrical, heating, or other mechanical systems

- Easements, common driveways, or fences

- Room additions, structural alterations, repairs, replacements, or other changes, especially those made without required building permits

- Flooding, drainage, or soil problems on, near, or in any way affecting the property

- Zoning violations, such as nonconforming uses or insufficient setbacks

- Homeowners' association obligations and deed restrictions or common area problems

- Citations against the property, or lawsuits against the owner or affecting the property

- Location of the property within a known earthquake zone

- Major damage to the property from fire, earthquake, or landslide

The written disclosure statement is required for any transfer by: sale, exchange, installment land sale contract, lease with an option to purchase, any other option to purchase, or ground lease coupled with improvements.

Property Transfers Requiring the Written TDS

- Sale

- Exchange

- Installment land sale contract

- Lease with an option to purchase

- Any other option to purchase

- Ground lease coupled with improvements

Property Transfers Exempt from the TDS Requirement

- Transfers pursuant to a court order

- Transfers by a foreclosure sale

- Transfers court-ordered by a fiduciary in the administration of a probate estate or a testamentary trust

- Transfers to a spouse or another related person resulting from a judgment of dissolution of marriage or of legal separation or from a property settlement agreement incidental to such a judgment

- Transfers from one co-owner to another

- Transfers by the state controller for unclaimed property

- Transfers resulting from the failure to pay taxes

- Transfers from or to any governmental entity

- Transfers of the first sale of a residential property within a subdivision and a copy of a public report is delivered to the purchaser or if such a report is not required

Timing of the TDS

A copy of the TDS must be provided to a buyer BEFORE an offer to purchase the property is presented.

If the real estate agent gives a copy of the disclosure statement to the buyer AFTER the offer to purchase the property is presented, the buyer may terminate the offer or agreement to purchase.

The buyer has 3 days after delivery of the disclosure in person or 5 days after delivery by deposit in the U.S. mail to terminate the offer to purchase.

Usually a listing broker obtains this statement at the time the listing is taken. If more than one real estate agent is involved in the transaction (unless otherwise instructed by the seller), the agent obtaining the offer is required to deliver the disclosure to the prospective buyer.

If the prospective buyer receives a report or an opinion prepared by a licensed engineer, land surveyor, geologist, structural pest control operator, contractor, or other expert (with a specific professional license or expertise), the liability of the seller and the real estate agents may be limited when making required disclosures.

A violation of the law does not invalidate a transfer; however, the seller may be liable for any actual damages suffered by the buyer.

Mello-Roos Assessment Disclosure

The **Mello-Roos Community Facilities Act** of 1982 authorizes the formation of community facilities districts, the issuance of bonds, and the levying of special taxes, which will finance designated public facilities and services.

A **Mello-Roos District** is an area where a special tax is imposed on those real property owners within a Community Facilities District. Public services (roads, sewers, parks, schools, and fire stations) in NEW DEVELOPMENTS may be financed under this law.

A Mello-Roos lien is placed on each parcel in a new development by the developer to pay off municipal bonds issued to fund off-site improvements for the development.

The developer must make the payments on the bond until the homes are sold, and then the new owners are responsible.

The seller of of residential property consisting of 1-to-4 dwelling units subject to a Mello-Roos lien must disclose if a property is subject to a Mello-Roos assessment and give a Notice of Special Tax to a prospective buyer.

If the Notice of Special Tax is delivered to the buyer AFTER a purchase agreement has been signed, the buyer has the right to terminate the agreement within 3 days of delivery in person, or 5 days after delivery by mail. The buyer must provide written notice of termination of the agreement to the seller or the seller's agent.

Prospective buyers must be told by real estate agents that a project is subject to a Mello-Roos special assessment because their tax bill will be higher than if they only paid property taxes without the special assessment. However, the listing agent does not have an affirmative duty to discover a special tax district or assessment not actually known to the agent.

Natural Hazard Disclosure Statement

Unless exempt, all sellers or sellers' agents must determine and disclose to prospective purchasers if a parcel is in certain officially mapped natural hazard zones (geologic, flood, and fire) by giving them a **Natural Hazard Disclosure Statement** (NHDS) if the residential property lies within any of six statutorily specified areas.

Areas Subject to NHDS Disclosures

1. **Special flood hazard** (Zone A or Zone V) area designated by the Federal Emergency Management Agency (FEMA).

2. **Area of potential flooding** in the event of a dam failure, designated by the California Office of Emergency Services.

3. **Very high fire hazard severity zone** designated by the California Department of Forestry and Fire Protection (CDF).

4. **Designated wild land fire area** that may contain substantial forest fire risks and hazards, designated by the State Board of Forestry.

5. **Earthquake fault zone** designated by the State Geologist.

6. **Seismic hazard zone** designated by the State Geologist.

The disclosure must be made as soon as practicable BEFORE the transfer of title, unless the purchase contract provides for an earlier deadline.

It is in the seller's and listing agent's best interest to disclose early because the buyer can annul the purchase contract during a certain period after getting the information.

The rescission period is 3 days if the disclosures are hand-delivered or 5 days if the disclosures are mailed.

The seller or his or her agent may have a third party consultant complete the NHDS in lieu of completing the NHDS themselves. However, using a third party consultant does not relieve the seller or his/her agent from the obligation to deliver NHDS to the buyer.

Areas Subject to NHDS Disclosures

Special Flood Hazard Area (Any type Zone "A" or "V")

Flood hazard boundary maps identify the general flood hazards within a community. They are also used in flood plain management and for flood insurance purposes.

The maps, developed by the **Federal Emergency Management Agency (FEMA)** in conjunction with communities participating in the National Flood Insurance Program (NFIP), show areas within a **100-year flood boundary**, termed SPECIAL FLOOD ZONE AREAS.

Also identified are areas between 100 and 500-year levels termed areas of moderate flood hazards and the remaining areas above the 500-year level termed areas of minimal risk.

A seller of property located in a special flood hazard area, or the seller's agent and/or any agent cooperating in the deal, must disclose to the buyer that federal law requires **flood insurance** as a condition of obtaining financing on most structures located in a special flood hazard area.

Since the cost and extent of flood insurance coverage may vary, the buyer should contact an insurance carrier or the intended lender for additional information.

The Local Option Real Estate Transfer Disclosure Statement (LORETDS) also lists disclosures, providing the local jurisdiction has mandated the use of this form.

Areas of Potential Flooding

Designated on an **inundation map** are areas that may flood as the result of a **dam failure**.

Seller/listing broker must disclose if the property is on a list posted at:

- County Public Works/Engineering Offices
- Assessors Office
- Water Agencies
- Planning Agency

If the owner has received federal flood disaster assistance, the seller must tell the buyer to buy flood insurance. This is disclosed on the NHDS.

State Fire Responsibility Areas

The Department of Forestry and Fire Protection has maps identifying rural lands classified as **state responsibility areas**.

In these areas, the state has the primary financial responsibility for the prevention and extinguishing of fires.

Maps of State Responsibility Areas and any changes, including new maps produced every five years, are to be provided to planning agencies in the affected counties.

The seller must disclose the possibility of substantial fire risk and that the land is subject to certain preventative requirements if the property is located in a state responsibility area, or if the property is included on a map given by the Forestry Department to the county assessor or planning agencies.

A county may assume responsibility for all fires, including those occurring in State Responsibility Areas.

If the county assumes this responsibility, the seller of property located in the area must disclose to the buyer that the state is not obligated to provide fire protection services for any building or structure unless such protection is required by a cooperative agreement with a county, city, or district.

Very High Fire Hazard Zone

The seller must disclose if the property is in a **very high fire hazard zone**. Properties in this zone are subject to property maintenance requirements, such as clearing brush and maintaining firebreaks.

Generally, a 30-foot clearance area is required around dwellings.

Designated Wildland Fire Area

A **designated wildland fire area** may contain substantial forest fire risks and hazards.

Earthquake Fault and Seismic Hazard Zones

The State Legislature passed two laws to protect public safety from the effects of surface fault rupture and seismic hazards caused by earthquakes—the Alquist-Priolo Earthquake Fault Zoning Act (1972) and the Seismic Hazards Mapping Act (1990).

These laws require the State Geologist to delineate various earthquake fault zones and seismic hazard zones.

The **Alquist-Priolo Earthquake Fault Zoning Act** prevents the construction of buildings for human occupancy on the surface trace of active faults. This Act only addresses the potential hazard of surface fault rupture and not other hazards associated with earthquakes.

> An **earthquake fault zone** is an area delineated by state officials to have an active fault within it and have the potential for surface rupture.
>
> Example: The 7.3 Landers earthquake (1992) created a 76-mile surface crack in the desert floor with as much as 18 feet of horizontal displacement and as much as 6 feet of vertical displacement. The surface fault rupture passed directly beneath/through a house in Landers splitting it apart.

The **Seismic Hazards Mapping Act** addresses non-surface fault rupture earthquake hazards, including liquefaction, lateral spreading, and seismically induced landslides. **Seismic hazard zones** are regulatory zones that have a potential for liquefaction or earthquake-induced landslides that may affect the property.

> Example: Serious soil liquefaction occurred in the Marina District of San Francisco during the 7.1 Loma Prieta earthquake (1989). The displacement of the ground underlying the Marina District caused the vertical settlement and lateral displacement of buildings as well as the buckling of sidewalks, the cracking of asphalt pavement, and the rupture of underground pipes.

These potential hazards must be disclosed upon sale of the property and must be evaluated prior to obtaining a building or grading permit.

The State geologist prepares and issues appropriate maps that are distributed to all affected cities, counties, and state agencies for their use in planning decisions.

Disclosing Earthquake Hazards on the HNDS

The fact that a property is located in an Earthquake Fault Zone or Seismic Hazard Zone must be disclosed to a potential buyer before the sales process is complete.

Disclosure must be made on:

- Natural Hazard Disclosure Statement (NHDS), or

- Local Option Real Estate Transfer Disclosure Statement (LORETDS).

Homeowner's Guide to Earthquake Safety Booklet

Real estate licensees are required to provide sellers with copies of the *Homeowner's Guide to Earthquake Safety* booklet.

A seller must deliver a copy of the *Homeowner's Guide to Earthquake Safety* booklet to buyers.

Additionally, the seller must complete the Residential Earthquake Hazards Report (found at the back of the booklet) prior to giving the booklet to the buyer.

Requirement: *Homeowner's Guide to Earthquake Safety* Booklet

- Transfer of any real property with a residential dwelling built prior to January 1, 1960 and consisting of one-to-four units any of which are of conventional light-frame construction.

- Transfer of any masonry building with wood-frame floors or roofs built before January 1, 1975.

If the buyer of real property receives a copy of the *Homeowner's Guide to Earthquake Safety*, neither the seller nor the agent is required to provide additional information regarding geologic and seismic hazards.

The Seismic Safety Commission also published the *Commercial Property Owner's Guide to Earthquake Safety* booklet, which sellers or sellers' agents provide to buyers of commercial properties.

Furnishing Controlling Documents of CIDs

The owner (other than a subdivider) of a separate legal share in a common interest development (CID) must give prospective buyers the controlling documents and financial statements concerning the CID.

Types of CIDs

- Condominium project
- Planned development
- Community apartment project
- Stock cooperative

Required Documents

- Copy of the governing documents of the development

- Statement regarding an age restrictions, if any

- Copy of the homeowners' association's most recent financial statement

- Amount of current regular and special assessments as well as any unpaid assessments, late charges, interest and costs of collection that are or may become a lien against the property

- Any information on any approved change in the assessments or fees not yet due and payable as of the disclosure date

- Preliminary list of construction defects if the association has commenced or plans to commence an action for damages against the developer

- Disclosure of any settlement agreement or other instrument between the association and the developer regarding construction defects

Timing

Within 10 days of a written request, the association must provide the required documents to the owner or as directed by the owner to another person.

Stigmatized Property

The most common properties associated with stigmatized property are those in which there have been murders, suicides, or criminal activity.

In California, sellers and their agents do NOT have to disclose the fact of any death that occurred on the property to the buyer if the death was **MORE THAN 3 YEARS BEFORE** the buyer made an offer to buy the property.

However, if a death occurs on a property within 3 years and the circumstances of that death are **material** (gruesome, offensive, or affected the reputation of the property), it must be disclosed.

> Since it is difficult to judge what is considered material, it is better to disclose a death if it occurred within the last 3 years and let the buyer decide if it is a material fact.

> Death of an occupant on the property may be disclosed on the Exempt Seller Disclosure form (ESD). The ESD is a C.A.R. created form used to document seller's responses to certain disclosures required by law (but not appearing on the statutory TDS) or by contract.

Owners and their agents **do NOT** have to disclose that an occupant of a property was living with human immunodeficiency virus (HIV) or died from AIDS-related complications. [Civil Code §1710.2(1)(B)].

Water Heater, Smoke Detector, and Carbon Monoxide Detector Compliance

By the close of escrow, the seller must comply with state and local laws that the water heater is braced and that the home has operable smoke detectors installed. Additionally, the seller must state whether the home has carbon monoxide dectectors installled.

Water Heater Bracing

The seller must provide a written certificate that the water heater(s) braced, anchored, or strapped in place to resist falling or horizontal movement due to earthquake motion. The minimum standard is found in the California Plumbing Code. The buyer must acknowledge receipt of the certificate with his or her signature and date.

Smoke Dectectors Installled

The seller must provide a written certificate of having operable smoke detector(s) approved and listed by the State Fire Marshal installed in the home. The buyer must acknowledge receipt of the certificate with his or her signature and date.

Carbon Monoxide Dectectors Installled

The **Carbon Monoxide Poisoning Prevention Act** requires that **carbon monoxide detectors** (CO detectors) must be installed in all dwelling units that contain a fossil fuel burning heater, appliance, or fireplace; or that have an attached garage. **Carbon monoxide** is an odorless gas produced whenever any fuel is burned.

The Consumer Product Safety Commission recommends installing a CO detector in the hallway near every separate sleeping area of the home. They must be installed in single-family homes by July 1, 2011 and by January 1, 2013 in multi-family residences.

Sellers must notify buyers on the Real Estate Transfer Disclosure Statement whether the property has carbon monoxide devices installed. No separate compliance certification is required.

Energy Conservation Retrofit and Thermal Insulation Disclosures

State law prescribes minimum energy conservation standards for all new construction.

Local governments also have ordinances that impose additional energy conservation measures on new and/or existing homes. Some local ordinances impose energy retrofitting as a condition of the sale of an existing home.

The seller and/or agent should disclose to a prospective buyer the requirements of the various ordinances, as well as who is responsible for compliance.

Federal law requires that a new home seller (including a subdivider) disclose in every sales contract the type, thickness, and **R-value** (resistance to heat loss) of the insulation that has been or will be installed.

Home Energy Rating System Booklet

Sellers and/or real estate agents may deliver the optional *Home Energy Rating System* informational booklet concerning the statewide home energy-rating program to buyers.

The delivery of this booklet is not mandatory; however, the information in the booklet is deemed adequate to inform the buyer about the existence of a statewide home energy-rating program.

The **HERS booklet** is part of the *Combined Hazards Booklet*.

Water-Conserving Fixtures Disclosure

Residential and commercial properties built prior to January 1, 1994 must be retrofitted with water-conserving plumbing fixtures. Beginning in 2014, any remodeling or building alterations will require the replacement of noncompliant plumbing fixtures.

Effective 2017, sellers of single-family residences will need to disclose whether the plumbing fixtures in their residences are water-conserving plumbing fixtures or noncompliant fixtures.

Notice of Supplemental Property Tax Bill

A seller or his or her agent must give prospective purchasers a **Notice of Supplemental Property Tax Bill**.

The notice informs purchasers that county assessors revalue real property at the time the ownership of the property changes.

Therefore, the buyer may receive one or two supplemental tax bills, depending on when escrow closes.

Disclosure of Sales Price Information

A broker must inform both buyer and seller, in writing, the sale price on a property within one month of close of escrow. The Escrow Closing Statement meets this requirement.

Notice of Negotiability of Commissions

A notice printed in at least **10-point type** stating that commissions are negotiable must be given to the person paying the real estate commission.

A broker can share his or her commission with an unlicensed buyer or seller if the broker discloses this to all parties.

Topic 6, Disclosures in Real Estate - Review
Multiple-Choice Questions

1. A private seller advertises a single-family home for sale "as is". Since the seller is not using the services of a real estate broker, the seller:
    a. has met the legal requirement of caveat emptor by putting the term "as is" in the newspaper advertisement.
    b. is not obliged to disclose any defects in the property because the property is being sold "as is".
    c. must give a Real Estate Transfer Disclosure Statement to prospective buyers.
    d. is not obliged to give a Real Estate Transfer Disclosure Statement to prospective buyers.

2. A Real Estate Transfer Disclosure Statement is required in the _____ of one-to-four residential units.
    a. sale
    b. lease
    c. foreclosure
    d. all of the above

3. During negotiations for the purchase of a house, seller Butler never informed buyer Wright that the house was served by a septic tank with a failed drainfield. Escrow closed, Wright moved in, and shortly thereafter discovered the problem with the septic tank. What recourse does Wright have?
    a. Revoke the offer
    b. Rescind the contract with Butler based on fraud
    c. Rescind the contract with the broker
    d. Sue the title company

4. Regarding environmental hazards on the property, the seller is required to:
    a. give a copy of the *Environmental Hazards* booklet to the buyer.
    b. disclose any known environmental hazards to the buyer.
    c. complete and give the Transfer Disclosure Statement to the buyer.
    d. do all of the above.

5. Seller Sam listed his newer ranch-style home built in 2002 with broker Bob. Regarding the lead based paint disclosure, Sam must:

   a. give the buyer the pamphlet, *Protect Your Family From Lead in Your Home*.

   b. complete statements verifying completion of the disclosure requirements.

   c. must give the buyers a 10-day opportunity to test for lead.

   d. do none of the above.

6. Broker Marshall took a listing on a home. When filling out the NHDS, which of the following would Marshall not include?

   a. Flood hazard

   b. Seismic hazard

   c. Mold hazard

   d. Fire hazard

7. When a condominium is sold, the seller must, upon request, provide to the buyer:

   a. CC&Rs.

   b. bylaws.

   c. financial statements.

   d. all of the above

8. Broker Fisher took a listing on a property where a person died from AIDS. Does Fisher have to disclose this information?

   a. Yes, Fisher must disclose all material facts.

   b. No, Fisher does not have to disclose this information.

   c. Yes, but only if the death was within the previous three years.

   d. No, the law does not allow this disclosure to be made.

9. All homes with a fossil fuel burning fireplace or an attached garage must:

   a. install carbon monoxide detectors.

   b. have braced water heaters.

   c. install operable smoke detectors.

   d. have water heater insulation blankets.

10. The law requires a seller to reveal any information that would be important to the buyer regarding the condition of the property in what document?

    a. Mello Roos Statement

    b. Statement of Compliance

    c. Transfer Disclosure Statement

    d. Pest Control Inspection Statement

11. What must be disclosed to purchasers under the Alquist-Priolo Special Studies Act?
    a. Location of toxic waste sites
    b. Water quality reports
    c. Location of flood hazard zones
    d. Location of earthquake fault lines

12. Special flood zone areas on the flood hazard boundary maps indicate that flooding occurs:
    a. every 50 years.
    b. within 100 years.
    c. within 100 and 500-years.
    d. over 500 years.

13. The Coopers closed escrow on a single-family home in February. After the close of escrow, they discovered they were responsible for:
    a. an increase in property taxes as a result of the sale, as well as the supplemental tax bill.
    b. no increase in taxes, but a supplemental tax bill for the following year.
    c. the former owner's back taxes.
    d. paying two year's taxes in advance.

14. Carbon monoxide detectors (CO detectors) must be installed in all dwelling units that contain a fossil fuel burning heater, appliance, or fireplace; or that have an attached garage—July 1, 2011 for single-family homes and January 1, 2013 in multi-family residences. What document does a seller use to disclose whether the property has carbon monoxide devices installed?
    a. Carbon Monoxide Disclosure Statement
    b. Real Estate Transfer Disclosure Statement
    c. Natural Hazard Disclosure Statement
    d. Poisonous Gasses Disclosure Statement

15. All of the following actions would be in violation of real estate law, except:
    a. a real estate broker sharing a commission with an unlicensed buyer if the broker discloses this to all parties.
    b. a licensed salesperson sharing a commission with another licensed salesperson.
    c. a licensed salesperson accepting commission from both principals to a transaction with the knowledge and consent of both principals.
    d. a broker sharing a commission with a licensed salesperson employed by another broker.

16. The R-value is a rating that measures:
    a. how well insulation resists heat.
    b. the efficiency of energy; used to determine the effectiveness of appliances.
    c. the amount of heat needed to raise one pound of water one degree Fahrenheit.
    d. insulation.

Answer Key

1. (c) The seller of a 1-4 unit residential property must complete and give a Transfer Disclosure Statement to a prospective buyer. A seller can sell a home "as is" but must still disclose any defects.

2. (a) The Transfer Disclosure Statement is required on a sale of 1-4 residential units. Choice (b) is not correct, because it must be a lease with an option of purchase.

3. (b) This is a material fact that should have been disclosed on page 1 of the TDS. If the offer had not been accepted, Wright could revoke his offer. Once escrow closed, Wright could rescind the sales contract based on fraud.

4. (d) The seller or seller's agent should give a copy of the Environmental Hazards booklet to the buyer. Additionally, the seller must disclose any known environmental hazards on the TDS and give it to the buyer.

5. (d) The home was built in 2002, so there is no disclosure requirement. This disclosure pertains to residential housing built before 1978.

6. (c) Choices (a), (b), and (d) are included on the Natural Hazard Disclsoure Statement (NHDS); mold is discussed on the Transfer Disclosure Statement (TDS).

7. (d) The owner must furnish the controlling documents, e.g., CC&Rs, bylaws, and the most recent financial statements.

8. (b) Neither the seller nor his or her agent has to disclose that an occupant of a property was living with human immunodeficiency virus (HIV) or died from AIDS-related complications. [Civil Code §1710.2(1)(B)].

9. (a) Carbon monoxide detectors (CO detectors) must be installed in all dwelling units that contain a fossil fuel burning heater, appliance, or fireplace; or that have an attached garage.

10. (c) The Transfer Disclosure Statement form requires sellers to disclose known property defects, which are not limited to the physical aspects of the property but also include items such as zoning violations and nuisances in the area.

11. (d) The Alquist-Priolo Special Studies Act requires the State Geologist to delineate various earthquake fault zones. An earthquake fault zone is an area delineated by state officials to have an active fault within it and have the potential for surface rupture.

12. (b) Special flood zone areas are areas within a 100-year flood boundary as indicated on flood hazard boundary maps.

13. (a) Upon the sale of real property, the property taxes will be assessed at 1% to 1.5% of the new purchase price. If the escrow closes between the time the seller has paid the taxes and new taxes are assessed the buyer also will receive a supplementary tax bill for the increase.

14. (b) Sellers notify buyers on the Real Estate Transfer Disclosure Statement whether the property has carbon monoxide devices installed.

15. (a) Answer (a) is the only one that is not in violation of the real estate law. Only brokers share commission, not salespersons. Only the broker accepts commission from one or more principals, not the salesperson.

16. (a) The R-value is a rating that measures how well insulation resists heat.

Topic 7, Escrow & Closing

In Topic 7, we will discuss proration, title insurance, legal descriptions, and tax issues in transferring real property.

An **escrow** is a small and short-lived trust arrangement. When ownership transfers from one person to another, usually a neutral third party, called an **escrow agent**, handling the details of the sale.

After escrow is opened, it is the escrow holder's job to follow the buyer's and seller's instructions and request all parties involved to observe the terms and conditions of the contract.

Two Basic Requirements for a Valid Sale Escrow

1. Binding contract between the buyer and seller

2. Conditional delivery of transfer documents and funds to a third party

The **binding contract** can be purchase agreement, agreement of sale, exchange agreement, option, or mutual escrow instructions of the buyer and seller.

A **conditional delivery** of transfer documents and funds means the:

- seller will deliver a signed instrument of conveyance (e.g., grant deed)

- buyer and/or the lender will deliver to escrow whatever funds are required for the sale.

Proration

When property is bought and sold, escrow charges certain expenses to each party in a process called proration.

Proration is the process of making a fair distribution of expenses, through settlement, at the close of the sale.

For prorating purposes, use 30 days for a month and 360 days in a year.

Review - Proration
The Proration Process

- Determine the number of days to be prorated

- Calculate the cost per day

- Multiply the number of days by the cost per day

- Decide whether the item should be a credit or a debit to the seller or to the buyer

- Expenses that have been paid to some time after escrow closes, credit the seller and debit the buyer.

- Expenses that will be due after the close of escrow, debit the seller and credit the buyer.

Commonly Prorated Items

- Property taxes

- Interest on assumed loans

- Fire and hazard insurance

- Rents

Title Insurance

In California, when escrow is opened, the escrow officer requests a **preliminary report** (prelim) from a title company.

A Preliminary Report:

- shows encumbrances, liens or any other items of record that might affect ownership.
  - ♦ It would show the existing seller's current loan or loans against the property. Therefore, the seller would appear as the trustor on the existing loan shown in the preliminary title report.

- is not a policy of title insurance but is only an offer to issue a policy of title insurance in the future for a specific fee.

- is used as the basis for the final title insurance policy.

- is the best source for the legal description of the property because all title insurance policies require legal descriptions.

Policies of title insurance are usually the standardized forms prepared by the **California Land Title Association (CLTA)** or the **American Land Title Association (ALTA)**.

The goal of title insurance companies is to ensure the clear, marketable title of property. **Marketable title** is one that a reasonable person would accept as clear and free from likely challenge.

The main benefit of title insurance is that it extends protection against matters of record and many non-recorded types of risks, depending on the type of policy purchased.

Two Types of Title Insurance Policies Normally Used In California
- Standard Policy of Title Insurance
- Extended Coverage Policy.

Legal Descriptions

In California, a valid deed does NOT have to have a legal description—it must have an ADEQUATE DESCRIPTION. However, it is prudent to have a legal description on a deed.

U.S. Public Land Survey System

In California, there are three intersecting baselines and meridians.

California Baseline and Meridian Starting Points
- Humboldt Baseline and Meridian (Northwestern California)
- Mt. Diablo Baseline and Meridian (Northeastern and Central California)
- San Bernardino Baseline and Meridian (Southern California)

Tax Issues in Transferring Real Property

Whenever property transfers to a new owner, real property is reassessed at 1% of fair market value, not necessarily the new sales price. Commonly, local taxes may be added to the 1% assessment. To estimate the amount of property tax that will be owed on a purchase, many people in the industry use 1.25% to account for local assessments.

Upon a change in ownership of real property, unless a statutory exemption applies, the property is reassessed based on 1% of the new purchase price, not accounting for local assessments. Statutory exemptions include transfers of real property between spouses or parents and children, and transfers for such purposes as correcting the names of the persons holding title. The complete list can be found on the websites of County Assessors.

> Example, if the sale price were $350,000, the new property tax would be $3,500. After that, a maximum increase of no more than 2% per year is allowed.

California Property Tax Calendar

A **fiscal year**, or tax year, is used for tax purposes as compared to a **calendar year**.

The fiscal or tax year starts on July 1 and goes through June 30 of the following year.

Taxation Time Line

Jan. 1	July 1	Nov. 1	Dec. 10	Feb.1	Apr. 10	June 30
taxes become a lien	tax year starts	1st installment due	1st installment delinquent	2nd installment due	2nd installment delinquent	tax year ends

On January 1, preceding the tax year, property taxes become a lien on real property.

The first installment is due November 1, but no later than December 10.

The second installment is due February 1, but no later than April 10.

Property Taxes are Due
Mnemonic - "NDFA"

No	November 1	(1st installment due)
Darn	December 10	(delinquent after this date)
Fooling	February 1	(2nd installment due)
Around	April 10	(delinquent after this date)

Special Assessments

When specific improvements that benefit a certain area are needed—such as underground utilities, sewers or streets—special assessments are levied to pay for them.

Difference between Special Assessments and Property Taxes

- Property taxes are used to operate the government in general.

- Special assessments are used for specific local purposes.

Special assessment liens are placed on the properties involved and usually paid at the same time as property taxes. The liens created by special assessments are equal in priority to general tax liens.

Street Improvement Act of 1911

The **Street Improvement Act of 1911** empowers cities and counties to levy a special assessment to repair streets. Each owner is assessed for the improvement based on the front footage of the property.

The amount of the assessment appears on the tax bill as a lien against the property. The assessment may be paid off at any time or paid in equal installments during the term of the bonds.

Mello-Roos Community Facilities Act of 1982

Mello-Roos covers a wide variety of community improvements, other than bond acts, for special assessments such as streets and sewers.

In some counties, Mello-Roos is on the tax bill, and in some other counties it is collected separately.

Topic 7, Escrow & Closing - Review
Multiple-Choice Questions

1. A small and short-lived trust arrangement is an.
   a. easement.
   b. encumbrance.
   c. escrow.
   d. exchange.

2. An escrow agent is authorized to:
   a. give the buyer advice about available financing.
   b. change the escrow instructions when asked to do so by the listing broker.
   c. call for funding of the buyer's loan.
   d. authorize a pest control company to make corrective repairs.

3. Prorations are part of closing costs. Which of the following items are always prorated?
   a. Property taxes and insurance
   b. Property taxes, insurance, and MMI
   c. Property taxes, insurance, PMI, and homeowners dues
   d. Property taxes

4. Buyer Ward assumed a note secured by a deed of trust. The balance of the note was $9,000 with an annual interest rate of 7 1/2% payable quarterly. The interest on the note was to be prorated upon possession of the property. The interest on the note was paid to March 31. If Ward took possession March 1, what would be his prorated interest owed, based on a 30-day month?
   a. $56.25
   b. $84.38
   c. $168.75
   d. $675.00

5. Escrow companies normally base their prorations on:
   a. 1 year.
   b. 360 days.
   c. 365 days.
   d. 12 months.

6. All of the following items are normally prorated at the closing, except:
    a. homeowner's insurance.
    b. property taxes and assessments.
    c. delinquent interest on unsecured loans.
    d. interest and impounds.

7. Kris owns a home that she agreed to sell to Dan. A preliminary report prepared during escrow, shows the:
    a. exact same information as found in Dan's future standard title policy.
    b. information about a deed of trust with Kris as trustor.
    c. new trust deed with Dan as trustor.
    d. title vested in Dan.

8. Which system of land description employs meridians and baselines?
    a. Metes and bounds
    b. Public Land Survey System
    c. Subdivision system
    d. Lot, block, and tract system

9. Referring to land descriptions:
    a. the Public Land Survey system, recorded track map or lot and block system, and metes and bounds are all considered legal descriptions.
    b. a Metes and Bounds description is not a measurement of land.
    c. the three intersections in the State of California are Humbolt, Mt. Diablo, and San Bernardino.
    d. all of the statements are correct.

10. Which of the following is an example of an ad valorem tax?
    a. Income tax.
    b. Estate tax.
    c. Bridge toll.
    d. Property tax.

11. What date does the first installment of real property taxes become delinquent?
    a. November 10
    b. December 10
    c. February 1
    d. April 10

12. The due date for the second installment of real property taxes is:
    a. November 10
    b. December 10
    c. February 1
    d. April 10

13. How do special property tax assessments differ from annual property tax assessments?
    a. Annual assessments have priority over special assessments.
    b. Special assessments are imposed only by local authorities.
    c. Judicial foreclosure is required for unpaid special assessments.
    d. Special assessments provide for local improvements.

14. The Street Improvement Act of 1911 allows the city or county to do all of the following, except to:
    a. put in sewers.
    b. improve sidewalks.
    c. install streetlights.
    d. buy additional land for development as subdivision.

15. Public services such as roads, sewers, parks, schools, and fire stations in new developments may be financed under:
    a. the Street Improvement Act of 1911.
    b. the Mello-Roos Community Facilities Act.
    c. Proposition 13.
    d. Proposition 60.

Answer Key

1. (c) An escrow is a small and short-lived trust arrangement.

2. (c) After escrow is opened, it is the escrow holder's job to follow the buyer's and seller's instructions and request all parties involved to observe the terms and conditions of the contract. Escrow agents may not offer legal advice, and may only act on written instructions from the parties to the escrow. Escrow agents write lenders of record for payoff amounts and funding. They accept pest control and similar reports, but cannot authorize any work.

3. (d) Even if a cash transaction, property taxes will always be prorated.

4. (a) One month's interest from March 1 to March 31. $9,000 x 0.075 = $675 per year divided by 12 months = $56.25/month.

5. (b) As a matter of convenience, escrow companies use a 30-day month, hence, a 360-day year.

6. (c) Interest on unsecured loans will not be prorated at closing.

7. (b) A preliminary report will show the existing loan with Kris as trustor.

8. (b) The Public Land Survey System uses imaginary lines to form a grid to locate land. North-south longitude lines, called meridians, and east-west latitude lines called baselines, intersect to form a starting point from which distances are measured.

9. (d) All statements of fact. Metes and Bounds is a method of land description, not measurement. The three intersections in the State of California are Humboldt, Mt. Diablo, and San Bernardino.

10. (d) Ad valorem means according to value and property is assessed according to its fair market value.

11. (b) First installment: Due on November 1st, delinquent on December 10th

12. (c) Second installment is due February 1, and delinquent if not paid on or before April 10.

13. (d) Special assessments are spent on specific local improvements such as streets, sewers, sidewalks, parks, and water supply and treatment. Only owners who are affected by the improvements pay the assessment.

14. (d) The Street Improvement Act of 1911 is used for street improvements. Each owner is assessed for the improvement based on the front footage of the property. According to the Street Improvement Act of 1911, cities and counties may not buy additional land for development.

15. (b) The Mello-Roos Community Facilities Act of 1982 authorizes the formation of community facilities districts, the issuance of bonds, and the levying of special taxes that will finance designated public facilities and services.

Topic 8, Real Estate Finance: Loans

In Topic 8, we will discuss California usury limits, title theory vs. lien theory states, default, foreclosure, and CalVet loans.

California Usury Limits

Usury is the charging of interest that is unreasonably high or beyond the legal limit set by the state. Usury laws are complicated and there are many exceptions to the general rules.

The California Usury Law makes a distinction between loans that are exempt from or covered by the law.

The usury laws do not apply to any real estate broker or mortgage loan originator if the loan is secured by real estate. This applies whether he or she is acting as a real estate broker.

The limitations also do not apply to seller carry back loans and to most lending institutions such as banks, credit unions, finance companies, pawnbrokers, etc.

Under the California Usury Law, the interest rate on a loan made primarily for personal, family, or household purposes cannot exceed 10% per year.

However, a loan used for home improvement or home purchase and all other loans made by a nonexempt lender are limited to the higher of 10% or 5% plus the discount rate charged by the San Francisco Federal Reserve Bank.

Title Theory States vs. Lien Theory States

California is a title theory state. It recognizes the lender as the owner of the property.

In a **title theory state**, title to real property is vested in the lender. In a title theory state, the mortgage states that title reverts to the borrower once the loan is paid.

In a **lien theory state**, title to real property is vested in the borrower. The borrower gives only a lien right to the lender during the term of the loan.

Whether the state is a lien theory or title theory state, possession of the property remains with the borrower.

Default and Foreclosure

Foreclosure is the legal procedure used by lenders to terminate all rights, title, and interest of the trustor or mortgagor in real property by selling the property and using the sale proceeds to satisfy the liens of creditors.

Two Ways to Foreclose—Trustee's Sale or by Judicial Process

- Any trust deed or mortgage with a **power-of-sale clause** may be foreclosed non-judicially by a trustee's sale or judicially by a court procedure.

- Without the power-of-sale clause, the only remedy a lender has is a judicial foreclosure by a court proceeding.

Most trust deeds and mortgages in California include the power-of-sale clause, so the lender may choose either type of foreclosure method.

Foreclosure on Trust Deed by Trustee's Sale (Non-judicial)

Usually the lender or noteholder will elect to foreclose on the loan using the trustee's sale because it is the quickest and easiest method taking APPROXIMATELY FOUR MONTHS.

Steps in a Trustee's Sale

First, the beneficiary (lender) notifies the trustor (borrower) of default and requests the trustee to record a **notice of default**. Anyone who has recorded a **Request for Notice** must be notified of the default.

The trustee must wait at least three months after recording the notice of default before advertising the trustee sale. Then the trustee advertises a Notice of Sale once a week for three weeks (21 days) and posts a notice of sale on the property.

As you can see the MINIMUM TIME between recording the notice of default and the trustee sale is THREE MONTHS AND 21 DAYS. During this time the trustor may **reinstate** (bring current) the loan up to 5 business days prior to the trustee's sale.

The trustee holds the sale and issues a **trustee's deed** to the highest bidder. A trustor has no right of redemption after the trustee sale.

If the proceeds of the sale are not sufficient to satisfy the debt being foreclosed, the noteholder may sue on the promissory note to obtain a deficiency judgment against the borrower. A **deficiency judgment** is a personal judgment against a borrower for the balance of a debt owed when the security for the loan is not sufficient to pay the debt.

However, the noteholder cannot obtain a deficiency judgment against the trustor under a trustee sale.

Foreclosure by Court Proceeding (Judicial)

Default on a mortgage, unless the mortgage includes a power-of-sale clause, requires a court foreclosure.

Steps in a Judicial Foreclosure

The mortgagee (lender) goes to court to start the foreclosure.

The court issues a decree of foreclosure and an order of sale.

After publication and posting of the sale notice, the court-appointed commissioner sells the property to the highest bidder and gives the buyer a Certification of Sale.

After a court foreclosure sale on a mortgage, the mortgagor (borrower) gets to keep possession of the property and has one year to redeem the property by satisfying the loan in full including court costs and any interest, unless the proceeds of the sale are sufficient to satisfy the secured indebtedness, then the redemption period is only 3 months. This is called **statutory redemption**.

If after one year (or 3 months), the mortgagor does not redeem the property, a **sheriff's deed** is issued to the new buyer.

If a trust deed is foreclosed in court, it is treated like a mortgage and the trustor (borrower) may keep possession during the redemption period.

Sometimes a lender with a trust deed may elect to foreclose by a court foreclosure. This may be the only way the beneficiary can obtain a deficiency judgment against the borrower.

Deficiency Judgments

A **deficiency judgment** is a personal judgment against a borrower for the difference between the unpaid amount of the loan, plus interest, costs and fees of the sale, and the amount of the actual proceeds of the foreclosure sale.

This means if the property sells for less than what is owed to the noteholder, the borrower will be personally responsible for repayment after the deficiency judgment is filed.

Deficiency Judgment Not Allowed

If a lender (beneficiary or mortgagee) chooses to foreclose a trust deed or mortgage with a power of sale using a trustee sale, no deficiency judgment is allowed if the proceeds do not satisfy the debt and all costs.

Since trust deeds are used almost exclusively in California to secure loans, the only security for a beneficiary is the property itself. Any other personal assets of the borrower in default are protected from judgment under a trust deed.

Additionally a lender cannot get a deficiency judgment against a borrower if the loan is a purchase money loan secured by either a trust deed or a mortgage.

Any loan made at the time of a sale, as part of that sale, is known as a **purchase-money loan**. This includes first trust deeds, junior loans used to purchase the property, and seller carry-back financing.

A seller is said to **carry back** when the seller extends credit to a buyer by taking a promissory note executed by the buyer and secured by a trust deed on the property being purchased as a part of the purchase price.

Deficiency Judgment Permitted

A deficiency judgment is allowed on hard money loans. A **hard money loan** is one made in exchange for cash, as opposed to a loan made to finance the purchase of a home.

Typically, a hard money loan refers to junior loans used to take money out for consumer purchases, home equity loans, debt consolidation, and even a refinance.

Government Backed Loans

There are two federal agencies and one state agency that help make it possible for people to buy homes they would never be able to purchase without government involvement.

The two federal agencies that participate in real estate financing are the Federal Housing Administration (FHA) and the Veterans Administration (VA).

The California Farm and Home Purchase Program, or CalVet loan is a state program that helps eligible veterans.

California Veteran Loans (CalVet)

The **California Department of Veterans Affairs** (Department) administers the **CalVet loan** program to assist California veterans in buying a home or farm.

Unlike other government financing, the CalVet program funds and services its own loans. Funds are obtained through the sale of State General Obligation Bonds and Revenue Bonds.

An eligible veteran (includes a 17-year old veteran) applies for the loan and makes loan payments directly to the Department of Veterans Affairs.

Overview of CalVet Loan Process

Veteran applies for a CalVet loan to the Department.

The Department approves the borrower and property

The Department purchases the property from the seller and takes title to the property.

The Department sells it to the veteran on a **contract of sale**. The Department holds legal title, with the veteran holding equitable title, until the loan is paid off and all the terms of the contract are met.

There are **no discount points** charged on a CalVet loan.

The veteran has an obligation to **apply for life insurance**, with the Department as beneficiary, to pay off the debt in case of the veteran's death.

Topic 8, Real Estate Finance: Loans - Review
Multiple-Choice Questions

1. Charging interest that is beyond the legal limit set by state law is called:
   a. discounting.
   b. hypothecation.
   c. proration.
   d. usury.

2. Seller Sam sold his home and carried back a $75,000 loan for 5 years at 12%. At the time of the sale, the discount rate charged by the San Francisco Federal Reserve Bank was 4%. Is this loan usurious?
   a. Yes, because it cannot exceed 9% based on the San Francisco Federal Reserve discount rate.
   b. No, because Sam is an exempt lender.
   c. Yes, because it exceeds 10%.
   d. No, because the usuary ceiling in Calfornia is 15%.

3. In a _____ theory state, title to real property is vested in the lender.
   a. title
   b. lien
   c. intermediate
   d. advanced

4. A mortgage creates a lien on real property or gives actual title to the lender depending on the laws of the state in which the property is located. In a _____ theory state, title to real property is vested in the borrower.
   a. loan
   b. lien
   c. title
   d. intestate

5. The two theories of how title follows a mortgaged property are _____ theory and _____ theory.
   a. modified / transfer
   b. lien / title
   c. trustee / trustor
   d. limited / periodic

6. Tracy recently closed on a purchase of a home, and her father is helping her prepare for the move. During a break, her father discussed the differences of mortgages. Especially, how legal title follows a real property. These theories ultimately depend on the state laws in which the property is located. Since Tracy's home is in a title theory state, who holds title?
   a. Title is vested in borrower
   b. Title is vested jointly
   c. Title is vested in the lender
   d. Title is vested in the trustee

7. Foreclosure of a deed of trust may be accomplished either by court action or by power of sale. Foreclosure by court action:
   a. is not a remedy available in California.
   b. prohibits a deficiency judgment.
   c. usually establishes a right-of-redemption period.
   d. is identical to foreclosure by trustee sale.

8. A property is in the process of foreclosure. If selling under the power of sale clause of a trust deed, the trustee must wait 3 months before:
   a. publishing a notice of intention to sell the property.
   b. publishing a notice of foreclosure on the property.
   c. recording a notice of default.
   d. evicting the owner from the property.

9. A power of sale or trustee's sale foreclosure of a purchase money deed of trust:
   a. is similar to a court foreclosure.
   b. prohibits a deficiency judgment.
   c. allows for no reinstatement period.
   d. gives the trustor rights of redemption.

10. Real property subject to a mortgage was foreclosed judicially. What is the maximum amount of time after the foreclosure of the sale that the mortgagor may remain in possession of the property?
    a. 30 days
    b. 90 days
    c. 180 days
    d. one year

11. Who would pay the discount points on a CalVet loan?
    a. Buyer
    b. Lender
    c. Seller
    d. No one

12. What type of security instrument does a veteran receive in a CalVet purchase?
    a. Mortgage
    b. Deed of trust
    c. Contract of sale
    d. Security deed

13. Which loan program requires the borrower to obtain life insurance?
    a. FHA
    b. VA
    c. Fannie Mae
    d. CalVet

14. Which agency holds the deed on a CalVet loan?
    a. Veterans Administration
    b. Department of Veterans Affairs
    c. FHA
    d. Freddie Mac

15. Funds used to finance the California Veterans Farm and Home Purchase Program come from:
    a. state funds backed by federal funds.
    b. state bonds.
    c. state reserves.
    d. state pension funds.

Answer Key

1. (d) Usury is the charging of interest that is unreasonably high or beyond the legal limit set by the state.

2. (b) Exempt loans include loans made by banks, savings and loans, and credit unions; real estate loans made directly or arranged by a mortgage loan broker; and seller carry back loans. However, a loan used for home improvement or home purchase and all other loans made by a nonexempt lender are limited to the higher of 10% or 5% plus the discount rate charged by the San Francisco Federal Reserve Bank.

3. (a) In a title theory state, title to real property is vested in the lender. In a title theory state, the mortgage states that title reverts to the borrower once the loan is paid.

4. (b) In a lien theory state, title to real property is vested in the borrower. The borrower gives only a lien right to the lender during the term of the loan.

5. (b) There are two theories of how title follows a mortgaged property—lien theory and title theory.

6. (c) In a title theory state, title to real property is vested in the lender. In a title theory state, the mortgage states that title reverts to the borrower once the loan is paid.

7. (c) A judicial foreclosure has a redemption period in which the borrower may buy back the property.

8. (a) When foreclosing on a trust deed under a power of sale, the lender (beneficiary) notifies the borrower (trustor) of default and requests the trustee to record a notice of default. The trustee must wait at least 3 months after recording the notice of default before advertising the trustee sale. The trustee advertises a Notice of Sale once a week for three weeks (21 days) and posts a notice of sale on the property. The trustee holds the sale and issues a trustee's deed to the highest bidder.

9. (b) A trustee's sale is a non-judicial sale. In a trustee's sale, no deficiency judgments are permitted on purchase money loans.

10. (d) The mortgagor may remain in possession for up to one year after the foreclosure sale, but must pay rent.

11. (d) There are no discount points charged on a CalVet loan.

12. (c) Department of Veterans Affairs purchases the property from the seller, takes title to the property, and sells it to the veteran on a contract of sale. The Department holds legal title, with the veteran holding equitable title, until the loan is paid off and all the terms of the contract are met.

13. (d) The veteran has an obligation to apply for life insurance, with the Department of Veterans Affairs as beneficiary, to pay off the debt in case of the veteran's death.

14. (b) The Department of Veterans Affairs holds legal title under a contract of sale.

15. (b) Funds are obtained through the sale of State General Obligation Bonds and Revenue Bonds.

Topic 9, Real Estate Finance: Lending Institutions

In Topic 9, there is no Calfornia-specific content.

Topic 10, Valuation & Appraisal

In Topic 10, there is no Calfornia-specific content.

Topic 11, Land Use, Subdivisions & Housing

In Topic 11, we will discuss California subdivision laws, housing, and construction.

California Subdivision Laws

California has two basic laws that control subdivisions—the **Subdivision Map Act** and the **Subdivided Lands Law**.

Subdivision Map Act

Under the **Subdivision Map Act**, the city or county is authorized to control the orderly and proper development of the community.

The Subdivision Map Act

- Directly controlled by local authorities (city and county)

- Concerned with the physical aspects of a subdivision
  - Building design

  - Streets

  - Any adverse effects to the environment

Subdivided Lands Law

The **Subdivided Lands Law** is directly administered by the Real Estate Commissioner—NOT local authorities.

Its objective is to protect buyers from fraud, misrepresentation, or deceit in the marketing of subdivided lots, parcels, units, and undivided interests in new subdivisions.

This even applies to LANDS OUTSIDE THE STATE, if they are being marketed in California.

An **undivided interest** is a partial/fractional interest in an entire parcel of land. The land itself has not been divided, but its ownership has been divided.

The creation, for sale, lease, or financing of 5 OR MORE undivided interests in land, whether or not improved, constitutes a **subdivision**.

Public Report

Before any subdivision can be offered for sale in California, the Real Estate Commissioner must determine that the offering meets certain standards and issue a public report.

The **public report** is a document disclosing important facts about the marketing and financing of the subdivision. These disclosures may alert a potential buyer to any negative aspects in the subdivision (e.g., natural or environmental hazards, unusual costs, restrictions, easements, or financing arrangements).

The public report must show that the subdivider (owner) can complete and maintain all improvements and that the lots or parcels can be used for the purpose for which they are being sold.

Preliminary Public Report

A developer may begin to market the properties before the issuance of a final public report by requesting a preliminary public report. A **preliminary public report** does not provide the same disclosures as a final report.

It allows the developer to ACCEPT RESERVATIONS from potential purchasers. Reservation money must be fully refundable and kept in an escrow. Preliminary public reports are issued for a one-year term and may be renewed.

Final Public Report

Before a subdivider can actually sell each lot in the project, he or she must give a copy of the Commissioner's **final public report** to the prospective buyer for approval.

The buyer signs a receipt for the report on a form approved by the Commissioner stating it has been read. The seller (subdivider) must **keep a copy of the statement for 3 years**.

The subdivider must post a notice in the sales office that says that a copy of the public report must be given to any member of the public who asks for it.

The final public report is **valid for 5 years** with any material changes in the development reported to the Commissioner, who then can issue an amended public report.

Housing & Construction

The housing and construction industries in California are regulated by three laws: the State Housing Law, local building codes, and the Contractors' State License Law.

The **State Housing Law** outlines the minimum construction and occupancy requirements for dwellings. Since 1970, the applicable building codes for the entire state are the Uniform Housing Code, Uniform Building Code, Uniform Plumbing Code, Uniform Mechanical Code, and National Electric Code.

Local government still has the power to set requirements for local zoning, local fire zones, building setbacks, side and rear yards, and property lines.

Whenever there is a conflict between public restrictions (e.g., zoning) and private restrictions, the *more restrictive* of the two must be followed.

The **Contractors' State License Law** licenses contractors in order to protect California consumers.

Topic 11, Land Use, Subdivisions & Housing - Review
Multiple-Choice Questions

1. The law giving the city or county authority to control the orderly and proper development of the community is called the:
    a. Subdivided Lands Law.
    b. State Housing Law.
    c. Subdivision Map Act.
    d. Contractors' State License Law.

2. The Subdivided Lands Law applies to a subdivision of _____ or more undivided interests in land.
    a. one
    b. two
    c. four
    d. five

3. It is said that the Commissioner's Public Report is the chief weapon against fraud in the sale of subdivided lands in California. All of the following are correct statements concerning the public report, except:
    a. a broker may take a listing on and show property before the issuance of the final public report.
    b. a preliminary public report issued by the Commissioner enables the subdivider to take reservations. However, it expires in one year.
    c. a final public report expires in 5 years.
    d. the option of 5 lots in a subdivision to one buyer does not constitute a material change in ownership.

4. Which of the following elements of a subdivision are regulated by local planning commissions under the state Subdivision Map Act?
    a. Physical aspects, such as streets and sidewalks, of an out-of-state subdivision
    b. Approval of the public report
    c. Verification that the subdivider has a valid license issued by the Bureau of Real Estate
    d. Assurance that adequate provisions have been made for sewage disposal and flood control.

5. According to the Subdivided Lands Law, what must the developer (seller) give a buyer before selling a lot in the subdivision?
    a. Grant deed
    b. Preliminary public report
    c. Final public report
    d. EIR

6. The Real Estate Commissioner's final public report expires:
    a. one year from the date of the report.
    b. never, unless a material change occurs.
    c. five years from the date of the issuance of the report.
    d. three years from the date of the issuance of the report.

7. The receipt for a final public report must be kept on file by the subdivider or his agent for a minimum of:
    a. one year.
    b. two years.
    c. three years.
    d. four years.

8. A developer of a new subdivision is giving potential buyers a preliminary public report. The preliminary public report allows the developer to:
    a. sell the homes.
    b. open escrow on the purchased homes.
    c. accept reservations for the homes.
    d. accept the down payment for the homes.

9. If the subdivision offering undergoes a material change, the subdivider must apply for:
    a. an interim report.
    b. an amended report.
    c. a conditional report.
    d. a preminimary report.

10. Which of the following statements is incorrect?
    a. State Housing Law has minimum construction requirements for houses.
    b. State building inspectors enforce the construction regulations.
    c. Local building inspectors enforce the construction regulations.
    d. Local health officers enforce the occupancy and sanitation regulations.

11. David plans to build an improvement that is regulated by the State Housing Act and by the local building codes. David must abide by:
    a. only local regulations.
    b. the contractor's license law.
    c. the State Housing Law that prevails over local ordinances.
    d. the more stringent of the laws.

12. The basic regulations of the housing and construction industries in this state are accomplished by the:
    a. State Contractors License Law.
    b. local building codes.
    c. State Housing Act.
    d. any or all of the above

Answer Key

1. (c) The Subdivision Map Act authorizes cities and counties to control the orderly and proper development of the community. The Real Estate Commissioner regulates the sale or lease of subdivided real property under the Subdivided Lands Law. Contractors are licensed in California under the Contractors' State License Law. The State Housing Law outlines the minimum construction and occupancy requirements for dwellings.

2. (d) The Subdivided Lands Law applies to a subdivision of five or more undivided interests in land.

3. (d) Answers (a), (b), and (c) are all correct statements. Answer (d) is not. This would constitute a material change.

4. (d) Out-of-state subdivisions sold in California come under the Subdivided Lands Law. Approval of the public report is done by the Commissioner. Answer (c) is not necessary at all.

5. (c) Before a subdivider can sell each lot in the project (subdivision), he or she must give a copy of the Commissioner's final public report to the prospective buyer for approval.

6. (c) Matter of law, unless there is a material change.

7. (c) A subdivider must keep a copy of the final public report for three years.

8. (c) A developer may begin to market the properties before the issuance of a final public report by requesting a preliminary public report. A preliminary public report does not provide the same disclosures as a final report and only allows the developer to accept reservations from potential purchasers.

9. (b) If during the life (five years) of a final public report, the subdivision offering undergoes a "material change" (e.g., change of ownership, change in purchase money handling procedure, change in use, etc.), the subdivider must apply for an amended public report.

10. (b) State Housing Law outlines the minimum construction and occupancy requirements for dwellings. Local building inspectors enforce the construction regulations while local health officers enforce the occupancy and sanitation regulations.

11. (d) The State Housing Law outlines the minimum construction and occupancy requirements for dwellings. If local building codes are more stringent than the minimum construction standards set by state law, David must comply with the local building codes.

12. (d) Answers (a), (b), and (c) all regulate the housing and construction industries in the state; therefore, answer (d) is the best answer.

Topic 12, Real Estate Brokerage

In Topic 12, we will discuss the legal status of a licensed salesperson, the employment agreement, and California fair housing laws.

Legal Status of a Licensed Salesperson

For purposes of CALIFORNIA REAL ESTATE LAW AND REGULATIONS, salespersons and broker-salespersons associated with a broker are **considered EMPLOYEES of the broker**.

This is because the broker is required by law to supervise the activities of the salesperson. However, the broker must have a written independent contractor agreement with each of his or her associate-licensees. This agreement allows the associate-licensees to be *self-employed*.

The broker-associate licensee employment relationship is viewed in this manner only by the license law not by other agencies. For ALL OTHER PURPOSES, salespersons and broker-salespersons associated with a broker **are considered SELF-EMPLOYED**.

Employment Agreement

The real estate law requires that every broker must have a **written employment agreement** with each of his or her salespeople, whether they are licensed as a salesperson or as a broker under a broker-associate arrangement.

Although the employment agreement does not have to be on a form approved by the Commissioner, it must cover the important aspects of the employment relationship.

Written Employment Agreement Must Cover

- Supervision of licensed activities

- Licensee's duties

- Compensation arrangement. A salesperson can only be paid by his or her employing broker. He or she cannot receive compensation or referral fees from a lender, developer, or seller.

Even though the IRS legally defines the associate-licensees as statutory non-employees, the C.A.R. employment agreement most commonly used is still called an Independent Contractor Agreement.

The agreement must be dated and signed by both parties and both the salesperson and the broker must keep copies of it for **3 years after termination of employment**.

If an employing broker and real estate salesperson meet the following tests, the broker is **not treated as an employer** and the salesperson is **not treated as an employee** for federal income tax purposes. The IRS legally defines the associate-licensees as **statutory non-employees**,

Tests Used to Determine Statutory Nonemployee Status

- The salesperson or broker-salesperson must be duly licensed;

- The salesperson or broker-salesperson must be compensated on the basis of the number of sales closed and commissions earned—not on the basis of the number of hours worked; and

- There must be a written contract between the broker and the salesperson providing that the salesperson will not be treated as an employee for federal tax purposes. 26 USC §3508

Statutory nonemployees are treated as *self-employed* for all federal tax purposes, including income and employment taxes.

Statutory nonemployees:

- must pay the full amount of Social Security and Medicare taxes, and not just a matching amount.

- receive 1099s (instead of a W-2 form) and must file a Schedule C to report their income and expenses.

- must make quarterly estimated tax payments. This does not necessarily increase the tax burden, unless payments are underestimated or late.

Fortunately, as a self-employed person, a salesperson or broker-salesperson has business deductions for various expenses that are not available to employees.

California Fair Housing Laws

California has enacted several laws and regulations to complement the Federal Fair Housing laws. However, California includes other protected classes to complement the protections of the federal law.

Protected Class	Federal Fair Housing Protections	California Fair Housing Protections
Race	X	X
Color	X	X
Religion	X	X
Sex	X	X
National Origin	X	X
Disability	X	X
Familial Status	X	X
Age		X
Ancestry		X
Marital Status		X
Sexual Orientation		X
Medical Condition		X
Source of Income		X
Genetic Information		X

California Fair Employment and Housing Act

The **California Fair Employment and Housing Act** (FEHA) is derived from an earlier law (**Rumford Act**) that dealt specifically with prohibiting discrimination in the sale, rental, or financing of practically all types of housing.

Currently, FEHA covers both housing and employment discrimination. Violations are reported to the state Department of Fair Employment and Housing.

Unruh Civil Rights Act

The **Unruh Civil Rights Act** (enacted in 1959) covers illegal discrimination in all business establishments—including real estate companies. The act specifically outlaws discrimination in housing and public accommodations based on sex, race, color, religion, ancestry, national origin, disability, medical condition, marital status, or sexual orientation.

It is particularly important for real estate licensees to be aware of the discriminatory practices of steering, blockbusting, and redlining.

> **Steering** is the illegal practice of only showing property in certain areas to buyers.

> **Blockbusting**, or causing **panic selling**, is the illegal practice of telling people that property values in a neighborhood will decline because of a specific event, such as the purchase of homes by minorities.

> **Redlining** is the illegal practice of disapproving real estate loans in economically or physically blighted areas.

Housing Financial Discrimination Act

The **Housing Financial Discrimination Act** (Holden Act) prohibits all financial institutions from discriminating in real estate loan approvals based on the geographic location, the neighborhood, or any other characteristic of the property.

In particular, redlining is forbidden unless it can be proved to be based on sound business practice. Violations may be reported to the state Secretary for Business and Transportation, who must act on the complaint within 30 days.

Topic 12, Real Estate Brokerage - Review
Multiple-Choice Questions

1. Which of the following statements is incorrect?
   a. The real estate license law considers a licensed salesperson an employee of the broker.
   b. For federal income tax purposes, the salesperson is considered an employee.
   c. Except for purposes of supervision under the license law, a salesperson is self-employed.
   d. The broker must pay workers' compensation for both clerical workers and sales associates.

2. Which of the following statements is correct regarding the basic tests used to determine statutory nonemployee status?
   a. The salesperson must have a valid California real estate license.
   b. The salesperson must be compensated on the basis of the number of sales closed and commissions earned—not on the basis of the number of hours worked.
   c. There must be a written contract between the employing broker and the salesperson specifying that the salesperson will not be treated as an employee for both federal and California tax purposes.
   d. All of the statements are correct.

3. Which statement is incorrect regarding the broker/salesperson employment agreement?
   a. The real estate law requires that every broker must have a written agreement with each of his or her salespeople.
   b. The employment agreement must be on a form approved by the Commissioner.
   c. Both parties must sign the employment agreement.
   d. After termination of employment, both broker and salesperson must keep copies of it for three years.

4. Even though sales associates are considered self-employed for federal and state income tax purposes, a broker must provide Workers' Compensation insurance for:
   a. all clerical workers.
   b. all sales associates.
   c. both (a) and (b).
   d. neither (a) nor (b).

5. The illegal practice of only showing property in certain areas to buyers is called:
    a. blockbusting.
    b. panic selling.
    c. redlining.
    d. steering.

6. Which California law covers illegal discrimination in all business establishments—including real estate companies?
    a. California Fair Employment and Housing Act
    b. Rumford Act
    c. Holden Act
    d. Unruh Civil Rights Act

7. A real estate licensee under California law should not take restrictive listings or advertise dwellings that suggest discrimination because of the:
    a. Code of Ethics.
    b. Fair Housing Amendments Act of 1988.
    c. Title VIII of the Civil Rights Act of 1968.
    d. Unruh Civil Rights Act

8. Which of the following is a federal law dealing with illegal discrimination in housing and financing?
    a. Fair Employment and Housing Act
    b. Fair Housing Act
    c. Housing Financial Discrimination Act
    d. Unruh Civil Rights Act

9. A salesperson is using strong efforts to obtain listings in a nonintegrated community. He finds success by insinuating that if minorities move in, the value of the property will decrease. His activities may be best described as:
    a. steering.
    b. panic peddling.
    c. blockbusting.
    d. both b and c

10. Causing panic selling by telling people that values in a neighborhood will decline because of a specific event is known as:
    a. steering.
    b. blockbusting.
    c. redlining.
    d. undervaluing.

11. Which of the following state agencies has the power to investigate and take legal action to prevent acts of discrimination in housing accommodations in California because of race, color, religion, national origin, or ancestry?
    a. Real Estate Commissioner
    b. State Department of Housing
    c. State Department of Labor
    d. Department of Fair Employment and Housing

12. If a person is in violation of the Rumford Act in refusing to sell property to a minority person, he could be made to:
    a. pay up to $10,000 in civil damages.
    b. sell the property to the individual if it is still available.
    c. sell a similar type property if he has a similar property for sale.
    d. any of the above

13. The illegal practice of telling people that property values in a neighborhood will decline because of a specific event, such as the purchase of homes by minorities is called:
    a. blockbusting.
    b. steering.
    c. redlining.
    d. panicking.

14. The California law that prohibits discrimination in the sale, rental or financing of practically all types of housing is called the:
    a. Holden Act.
    b. Housing Financial Discrimination Act.
    c. California Fair Employment and Housing Act.
    d. Unruh Civil Rights Act.

15. A mortgage loan broker took a home loan application from Mike and Mary Ito for a home in an older "up and coming" part of town. The sales price is at the high end of their budget and the home will need some renovation due to its age and condition. Mike and Mary recently graduated and Mike has been working in his chosed field for 8 months. Unfortunately, Mary could only find part time work. They have credit scores of 580 and 670 respectively and enough money saved for a 5% down payment. After analyzing their information, the lender disapproved a loan for Mr. and Mrs. Ito. Which statement is most likely correct regarding the lender's action?

    a. The lender is redling, which violates the Housing Financial Discrimination Act.

    b. The lender could deny the loan based on the low credit scores and lack of employment history.

    c. This is clearly discrimination based on ancestry.

    d. The Housing Financial Discrimination Act can force the lender to make the loan regardless of the creditworthiness of the potential borrowers.

Answer Key

1. (b) The license law considers a salesperson an employee, For income tax purposes, the IRS classifies real estate licensees as statutory nonemployees.

2. (d) The three answers correctly list the three requirements.

3. (b) The employment agreement does not have to be on a form approved by the Real Estate Commissioner.

4. (c) Due to their employee status, a broker must provide workers compensation coverage to all sales associates as well as any non-licensee employees of the firm.

5. (d) Steering is the illegal practice of only showing property in certain areas to buyers.

6. (d) The Unruh Civil Rights Act covers illegal discrimination in all business establishments—including real estate companies. The act specifically outlaws discrimination in housing and public accommodations based on sex, race, color, religion, ancestry, national origin, disability, medical condition, marital status, or sexual orientation.

7. (d) The Unruh Civil Rights Act covers illegal discrimination in all business establishments—including real estate companies. The act specifically outlaws discrimination in housing and public accommodations based on sex, race, color, religion, ancestry, national origin, disability, medical condition, marital status, or sexual orientation.

8. (b) The California Fair Employment and Housing Act (Rumford Act), the Unruh Civil Rights Act, and the Housing Financial Discrimination Act (Holden Act) are California laws that prohibit illegal discrimination in the sale, rental, or financing of practically all types of housing. The Fair Housing Act is a federal law.

9. (d) This would be both panic peddling and blockbusting.

10. (b) Blockbusting is persuading an owner to sell or rent housing by saying that people of a particular race, religion, etc., are moving into the neighborhood.

11. (d) The California Fair Employment and Housing Act (FEHA) is derived from an earlier law (Rumford Act) that dealt specifically with prohibiting discrimination in the sale, rental, or financing of practically all types of housing. Violations are reported to the state Department of Fair Employment and Housing.

12. (d) The Department of Fair Employment and Housing will investigate and can order the owner to sell or rent the unit to the complainant; offer to the complainant the next available unit; or pay civil damages up to $10,000 ($25,000 if there has been a prior violation).

13. (a) Blockbusting or panic selling is illegal. Steering is the illegal practice of showing clients property in only certain areas. Redlining is the illegal use of a property's location to deny financing.

14. (c) The California Fair Employment and Housing Act (Rumford Act) prohibits discrimination in the sale, rental or financing of housing. Housing Financial Discrimination Act (Holden Act) prohibits discrimination in real estate lending. The Unruh Civil Rights Act covers discrimination in business.

15. (b) The Housing Financial Discrimination Act prohibits all financial institutions from discriminating in real estate loan approvals based on the geographic location, the neighborhood, or any other characteristic of the property. In particular, redlining—the practice of disapproving real estate loans in economically or physically blighted areas—is forbidden unless it can be proved to be based on sound business practice.

Topic 13, Real Estate Specialization

In Topic 13, we will discuss the licensing requirements (and exemptions) for property managers and their employees.

Most people obtain a real estate license to sell homes; however, many other opportunities in real estate—such as property management—can be pursued.

Property Management

Any person who solicits for prospective tenants, negotiates leases, or collects rents from real property on behalf of an owner, must have a real estate license. However, there are some exceptions to this requirement.

Exemptions from the §10131 Licensing Requirement

- Resident manager of an apartment building and the employees of that manager

- Any employee of the property management firm retained to manage a residential apartment building (other than the resident manager and his/her employees) who is performing any of the following functions under the supervision of a broker of record who is an employee of that property management firm:

  (A) Showing rental units and common areas to prospective tenants.

  (B) Providing or accepting preprinted rental applications, or responding to inquiries from a prospective tenant concerning the completion of the application.

  (C) Accepting deposits or fees for credit checks or administrative costs and accepting security deposits and rents.

  (D) Providing information about rental rates and other terms and provisions of a lease or rental agreement, as set out in a schedule provided by an employer.

  (E) Accepting signed leases and rental agreements from prospective tenants.

Topic 13, Real Estate Specialization - Review
Multiple-Choice Questions

1. Tammy is employed as the resident manager of a 20-unit apartment house where she resides. Of the following statements, which is correct?
   a. Tammy is exempt from needing a real estate licence, but she will need a business license.
   b. As a resident manager, she is exempt from real state licensure.
   c. As a resident manager, she needs a real estate license to manage 16 or more units.
   d. Tammy is acting as an independent contractor and must obtain a property manager permit from the city.

2. Robert works for the broker of a property management company where he routinely solicits for prospective tenants, negotiates leases, or collects rents from properties.
   a. Robert is performing activities that require a real estate license.
   b. Robert is performing activities that do not require a real estate license.
   c. Robert works for the property management company and does not need a real estate license.
   d. Robert must have broker license in order to negotiate leases.

3. Sally works for a very large, privately held multi-family real estate company in Southern California. Which of the following tasks, if any, would require Sally to have a real estate license?
   a. Showing rental units and common areas to prospective tenants.
   b. Accepting signed leases and rental agreements from prospective tenants.
   c. Negotiating rental agreements with prospective tenants.
   d. Providing information about rental rates and other terms of a lease agreement, as set out in a schedule provided by an employer.

4. Real estate brokers, Sam and his sister, own a successful property manager company for which he is the broker of record. In addition, Sam has several income properties of his own. For which activities does Sam not need a real estate broker license?
   a. Collecting rents from real property on behalf of an owner.
   b. Soliciting prospective tenants for a property on behalf of an owner.
   c. Collecting rents from real property he owns.
   d. Negotiating leases for real property on behalf of an owner.

5. Any person acting as a property manager for another must have a real estate license unless he or she:

   a. is a resident manager of an apartment building.

   b. is the employee of a resident manager of an apartment building.

   c. is showing rental units and common areas to prospective tenants, while under the supervision of a broker of record employed by a property management firm.

   d. is performing any of the above-mentioned activities.

Answer Key

1. (b) A resident manager of an apartment building and the employees of that manager are exempt from licensing.

2. (a) Any person who solicits for prospective tenants, negotiates leases, or collects rents from real property on behalf of an owner, must have a real estate license. Robert must have a real estate license. However, he is not required to have a broker license as long as his salesperson license is held by an actively licensed real estate broker.

3. (c) The activities in choices "a", "b", and "d" are exempt from licensing.

4. (c) Any person who solicits for prospective tenants, negotiates leases, or collects rents from real property on behalf of an owner, must have a real estate license.

5. (d) All the the activities are exempt from licensing.